WORKHOLDING IN THE LATHE

FOR HOME MACHINISTS

WORKHOLDING IN THE LATHE

FOR HOME MACHINISTS

Workshop Practice Series

TUBAL CAIN

Technical Reviewer,
Paul Fiege

© 1990, 1994, 2000, 2005, 2007, 2008, 2010, 2012, 2016, 2019, 2025 by
Tubal Cain and Fox Chapel Publishing Company, Inc.

All rights reserved. *Workholding in the Lathe for Home Machinists* is a revised edition of *Workholding in the Lathe*, published in the UK in 2005 by Special Interest Model Books.

Technical Reviewer: Paul Fiege, CNC Machinist Faculty, Minneapolis Community and Technical College

ISBN 978-1-4971-0525-6

Library of Congress Control Number: 2025936539

To learn more about the other great books from Fox Chapel Publishing, or to find a retailer near you, call toll-free at 800-457-9112 or visit us at *www.FoxChapelPublishing.com*.

We are always looking for talented authors.
To submit an idea, please send a brief inquiry to acquisitions@foxchapelpublishing.com.
Or write to:
Fox Chapel Publishing
903 Square Street
Mount Joy, PA 17552

Printed in China

© Special Interest Model Books
An imprint of Fox Chapel Publishers International Ltd.
20-22 Wenlock Road
London
N1 7GU

www.foxchapelpublishing.co.uk

First published 2025
Text copyright 2025 Tubal Cain
Layout copyright 2025 Special Interest Model Books

ISBN 978-0-85242-908-2

Tubal Cain has asserted his right under the Copyright, Design and Patents Act 1988 to be identified as the author.

All rights reserved. No part of this publication may be reproduced in any form, by print, photography, photocopying, microfilm, electronic file, online or other means without written permission from the publisher.

Printed and bound in China

Because working with lathes and other materials inherently includes the risk of injury and damage, this book cannot guarantee that creating the projects in this book is safe for everyone. For this reason, this book is sold without warranties or guarantees of any kind, expressed or implied, and the publisher and the author disclaim any liability for any injuries, losses, or damages caused in any way by the content of this book or the reader's use of the tools needed to complete the projects presented here. The publisher and the author urge all readers to thoroughly review each project and to understand the use of all tools before beginning any project.

Contents

PREFACE		7
CHAPTER 1	**Between centers** Principles – conditions for accuracy – types of centers – centering the work – driving – non-circular workpieces – crankshafts – clamps and throwpieces – taper turning – mandrels.	8
CHAPTER 2	**Faceplate work** Principles and clamping – dogs – adhesive fixing – vee-blocks – fixtures – centering methods.	28
CHAPTER 3	**Chuckwork – General** Chucking principles – distortion – number of jaws – chuck mounting.	41
CHAPTER 4	**The Universal or Independent Chuck** Gripping forces – setting-up – irregular shapes – overhang – unorthodox methods – compound chucking.	47
CHAPTER 5	**The Self-centering Chuck** History – types – strength of the scroll – accuracy – the 'Griptru' – errors and wear – eccentric work – 4- and 6-jaw types.	57
CHAPTER 6	**Unusual Chucks** Bell and cup chucks – master-and-slave chuck – wood-block chucks – the shellac chuck.	71

CHAPTER 7	**Collets** Draw-in collets – dead-length types – double-taper and Schaublin collets – precautions – stepped collet chucks – auxiliary collets – arbors – adapters – deadstops – the Myford system.	78
CHAPTER 8	**Work Steady Rests** Principles – chatter – overhang – setting the fixed steady rest – boring in the fixed steady rest – setting the traveling steady rest – use with over-length work – the boring collar.	90
CHAPTER 9	**Lathe Alignment** Principles – lathe bench or stand – jacking screws – setting up with spirit level – the dial indicator method – the turning test method – caliper method – making a test-bar – alignment of a worn lathe.	101
INDEX		110

A Note on the Technical Review

Reviewing this title was interesting. I have been in the industry so long that I would have probably taken a different approach to machining at home, but it is insightful to read and understand that there are people out there with a little bit more creativity than me. This book truly deals with a lot of fundamentals of machining, and, as I usually tell my students, the fundamentals are the same as they were 100 years ago. It is the machines we use that can improve efficiency. This book is set up for home shop environments where efficiency is not an absolute must, so it helpfully references machines that are of the smaller variety and deals with the limits of those pieces of equipment.

—Paul Fiege
CNC Machinist Faculty
Minneapolis Community and Technical College

Preface

The center-lathe is by far the most versatile machine tool that we have – there is very little that it cannot do. Indeed, a considerable number of books have been written – going back nearly 200 years – explaining how to carry out work other than 'turning' on the lathe, and many of the now common machine tools owe their derivation to it. Even when using it for its proper purpose, however, problems arise as soon as we depart from plain turning between centers – and difficulties can arise even then. These are almost universally concerned with 'how to hold the work'. This book is intended to go some way to meet these problems.

Much that I have written is 'well-known', but I have included it because everyone has to begin somewhere, and when writing a book the beginning is no bad place to start! More important, many common practices are 'much used but little understood' and I hope that the explanations I have given as to WHY these methods are used may help the reader to overcome the difficulties he faces when the odd out of the ordinary workpiece appears. If the principles behind the various methods are understood, then it becomes a simple matter to invent new methods to do the old jobs better.

Most of the book is concerned with the actual holding of the workpiece, but I have added a short chapter covering the setting up of the lathe itself. No matter how carefully the workholding arrangements are made, if the lathe is not correctly aligned in the first place accuracy cannot be expected. Again, I have tried to explain *why* the machine must be set up as well as how, for there may well be better and simpler methods come to mind.

There is one area which I have NOT attempted to cover – that of 'Ornamental Turning'. This, the most highly developed form of the 'Art and Mystery of Turning', stretches the versatility of the lathe right to the limit – some would say well beyond that! The workholding devices needed are special in the extreme; if you are an Ornamental Turner you will have them or have made them, but if you are not, the mere sight of some of them would frighten you to death. So, I have directed my efforts solely to holding the work which any contracting or amateur center-lathe turner may expect to meet. I hope that what I have written will be of help to you.

Tubal Cain
Westmorland, Cumbria
August, 1986.

CHAPTER 1

Between Centers Work

'The work should be supported between centers' says one of my old textbooks. But what do we mean by 'support' – for this is the crux of the matter? See Fig. 1a. Here we have a 'something' in free space. It can move in the direction AA, sideways, BB, back-to-front, or CC, up-and-down. In technical terms it has 'three degrees of freedom'. It can be held still, of course, by 'gripping' it; in a vise or chuck, or with clamps, but this is *not* 'supporting' it. This term implies NO grip, and it is partly the absence of grip which makes between centers work so accurate. To 'support' the work free from movement we must apply stops as shown in Fig. 1b. If these no more than *touch* the work, then no translatory movement along any of the three axes can occur. We have 'supported' it. Note that we need six supports to cope with the three degrees of freedom.

Unfortunately this is not the whole story – see Fig. 1c. As well as moving in 'translation', as Fig. 1a, the object can *rotate,* and rotate abut the three axes we had before. It has three more degrees of freedom which we must cope. At first sight the stops of Fig.

1b. might prevent this rotation, but in fact it would be very unstable – especially with some more extreme shapes. So, we must provide supports in addition to those in Fig. 1b, as shown in Fig. 1d. You will see that three of each of the original stops is opposed by *two* stops, in the same plane, but spaced. Thus A and a1, a2, prevent rotation about the axis CC as well as restraining lateral movement along the axis AA; and so on. We now have nine stops to constrain six degrees of freedom; this is the minimum number of constraints which will hold a free body exactly in place, and they can do this without exerting any pressure at all (other than that due to the body's weight, of course). The piece will not be subject to any distortion due to clamping or gripping – a property that jig & tool designers make use of all the time.

To hold a body rigidly in place without gripping is, therefore, simply a matter of proper support. However, what happens if we want it to *move,* but in one axis only? In lathe work we are not concerned with moving the work in translation – *along* the axes – but we do require it to rotate or we could not

8 WORKHOLDING IN THE LATHE FOR HOME MACHINISTS

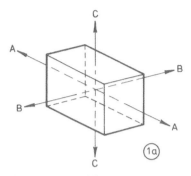

Three degrees of freedom — translation or linear movement

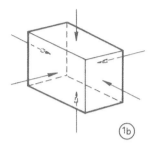

Complete constraint against linear movement.

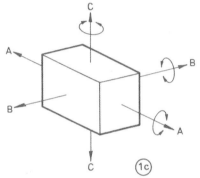

Three more degrees of freedom — in rotation

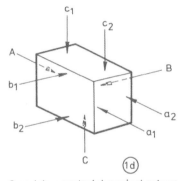

Complete constraint against rotary and linear movement.

Fig. 1

machine it. Let AA be the axis of rotation; very well – we must obviously remove the constraints b1, b2, c1 and c2, and B and C as well. It can now rotate about AA, but unfortunately we have left it free to move in translation along the TWO axes B and C, *and* it can also rotate about C. This clearly will not do! So we must find a device which still applies support against five of the six degrees of freedom which offers no constraint in the sixth – the axis AA. There are a number such. Bearings, for example. But if we are to use a bearing surface on the workpiece we must first machine it, and this we can not do until we have 'supported' it.

Fortunately a very elegant and mathematically sound method was discovered many thousands of years ago – long before the mathematicians had analyzed the problem. (Before any such existed, indeed, as so often happens in engineering!) If we apply a *pointed* support, engaging in a small hole in the workpiece at each end of the desired axis of rotation – Fig. 2 – this will do the trick. The two points – centers – acting

Between Centers Work 9

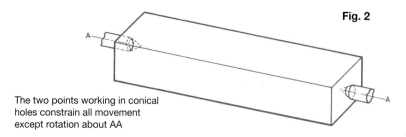

Fig. 2

The two points working in conical holes constrain all movement except rotation about AA

together can, *without exerting any force,* effectively prevent translation in any direction, and resist the rotation of the workpiece on the other two axes. Further, provided the points fit the holes in which they are engaged, the work can be removed and replaced with absolute exactitude – the setting is 'repeatable', and almost perfectly so. More than that. Provided the two points are identical in shape, and fit the holes properly, the work can be turned end-for-end in the machine and it will still revolve about exactly the same axis as before. The problem is solved.

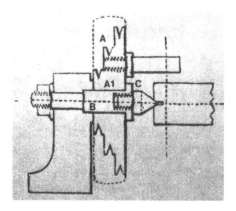

Fig. 3 *An early form "Dead Center" headstock drive. The pulley (A or A1) runs on the pin (B) which carries the center (c). (Holtzapffel Vol. IV fig. 39)*

Dead Centers

This is the term given to an arrangement where both centers (points) are held stationary in their supports – headstock and tailstock. The work revolves about both, being driven from the headstock end by means of a driver which rotates on a bearing surrounding the center. Fig. 3 shows an early example, with the cone pulley rotating on a fixed spindle. (Note that – as was common on early machines – the center is *screwed* in place instead of having the now more usual taper socket.) This system, much refined, is used today on all precision cylindrical grinding machines, and for very delicate work on watchmaker's lathes, but seldom on the ordinary engineer's lathe. A very high degree of both accuracy and repeatability is obtainable, but the complexity of the driving arrangement at the headstock makes it very expensive.

The Live Center

In this arrangement the center rotates with the work. In the normal center-lathe (with a few special exceptions, where the work is very heavy indeed) only the headstock center revolves, that at the tailstock still being a 'dead' or stationary center. We immediately come up against the fact that (a) unless the live center runs exactly true the work will rotate eccentrically; further, (b) if we take it out of the machine and

10 WORKHOLDING IN THE LATHE FOR HOME MACHINISTS

replace it, true repeatability will be impossible. The problem increases considerably in cases where *both* centers revolve. We shall return to this again later.

The important point to remember is that the centers should be no more than 'supports' as defined earlier, exerting pressure only when the machine is cutting and the tool-force has to be resisted. Care and judgement is needed when adjusting the fixed center at the tailstock; the work must be free, but with no shake. If pressure *is* exerted in the axial direction (in the absence of cutting load) then the workpiece will be stressed axially. Inevitably some distortion will result, especially if the work is slender. Now, as the machining proceeds, work is done on the metal and a fair amount of heat will be generated, so that the work will expand endways. If the principle of 'support' is to be maintained this must be compensated for – by readjustment of the tailstock. If this is not done there will be two consequences; first, the work will tend to spring into the shape of a bow (very slightly, perhaps, but this is a common cause of tool chatter) and, second, the pressure on the tailstock center will drive out the lubricant and, in the extreme case, overheat and draw the temper.

Conditions For Accuracy

(1) *Live, or Headstock center.* This must run true, as has already been mentioned. Fig. 4 shows the effect. The work and center rotate together, and the effect of an offset center will be as shown at 'a'. The work will still be truly circular, but the center of the workpiece A-A will not coincide with the axis of the center itself. If we now turn the work end-for-end, then the work will rotate

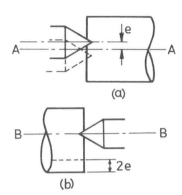

Fig. 4 *Effect of an untrue live center (a) The headstock center is offset, but the work is still truly round about the axis AA (b) Transferred to the tailstock the work rotates about BB, and is eccentric.*

eccentrically at the tailstock – see 'b'. This being so, the fixed center is always unhardened, and it must be corrected for truth every now and again – they always suffer some damage, if only from storage. It is also clear that the accuracy of the center will depend on the accuracy of the taper hole in the headstock spindle. The lathe manufacturer can be depended upon to see that this is right (if not, then do not buy that sort of lathe!) but the user must play his part. The taper socket must be kept scrupulously clean and no, *absolutely* no, accessory should be fitted in the headstock taper which can rotate within it and so cause scoring. A drawbar should *always* be used with, e.g., boring heads, drill chucks, and so on. If by some mischance the taper socket has been so damaged – with a very old lathe, for example – then it must either be rebored or, as an alternative, the headstock center must be retrued every time it is replaced. It is fairly important that the angle of the point of the center be correct – or at least uniform from one to another. As we shall see later, almost all such are made with a 60 deg. included angle, and some lathes I have seen had dowel pegs for setting over the topslide to exactly the right angle. Most modern machines have a scale of degrees which can be used instead, but some care is needed in the setting.

The headstock center should always be very slightly oiled when fitting, and it should be pressed home, not driven in with a mallet. The first application of the tailstock pressure should be used to drive home both centers – it will be found that they almost always retreat a little when pressure is applied; a movement axially of about a sixteenth of an inch is needed to squeeze out an oil film half a mil thick on a No. 2 Morse Taper.

(2) *Dead, or Tailstock center.* This is, of course, hardened, to withstand the wear involved. Like the headstock center, it must be truly axial, and the same remarks apply so far as the taper socket is concerned. Here, however, it is a comparatively easy matter to replace, so that drill chucks and even drills may be used without drawbars. On the other hand, it is *not* easy to re-form a damaged center point unless one has access to grinding equipment. Careful storage to avoid chipping the point is, therefore, essential. More common causes of damage, however, are overheating and grooving. The former kind of damage can be reduced by using High-speed Steel centers – my own practice – or even those with tungsten carbide tips. HSS is *not* harder than hardened carbon steel, but it does withstand heat better. Scoring is almost always caused by dirt in the center hole, though it can be the result of lack of lubrication.

Opinions differ as to the best lubricant. For over forty years I used common tallow – cheap and effective. When heavy cuts were expected I used to sprinkle powdered graphite on as well, to give some additional 'dry' lubricating qualities. More recently I have been using the molybdenum disulphide 'additive' which some misguided people put in their car engine sumps, used neat. I am not sure that I have noticed any advantage! The main point is to keep the center well lubricated – after all, it takes only the odd second to relax the tailstock between cuts and apply a little more oil; this is also an opportunity to adjust the tailstock pressure. In which connection, note that it is just as necessary to *close up* the tailstock if the work cools down – say when changing from roughing to finishing cuts.

(3) *Center Alignment.* This is a matter for the tailstock, but I am going to deal with it nevertheless. When handrest turning it does not matter very much if the head- and tailstock centers are not truly aligned to the axis of the bed, but when the tools are held rigidly in a slide rest which is guided by the bed, then it is imperative that they be true. See Fig. 5. If the two centers are not in line in the horizontal plane the effect is to turn the work taper, the taper on the diameter being twice the offset of the two centers. We can make use of this when we want to turn a tapered workpiece, of which more later, but it is otherwise a nuisance. I shall deal later with the methods of setting up a lathe to turn truly, (See Chap. 9).

Misalignment in the vertical direction is very uncommon indeed, but I have met this case in a very old machine. It is difficult to correct but fortunately has little effect on the diametral accuracy; a

12   WORKHOLDING IN THE LATHE FOR HOME MACHINISTS

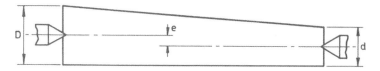

Fig. 5 *Effect of offset tailstock center. The work is round, but taper, so that $D = d + 2e$.*

vertical error of 1/64 in. may cause a taper of about 0.0004 in. per foot on a 1 in. dia. workpiece. There is, however, another consequence of misalignment, equally serious whether lateral or vertical. If the tailstock axis is not exactly in line with that of the headstock, any combination center drill (Slocombe drill) used from the tailstock is likely to be broken off at the point, and normal drills will tend to 'wander'. (4) *Fit of center profile*. The last of the conditions required to ensure accuracy is that the shape of the centers should correspond to that of the holes into which they operate. This is much more important when doing re-machining work than when starting from the beginning; a 90 deg. point, for example, will soon 'bed down' into a 60 deg. hole, and any shift of the axis of the workpiece in the process will be corrected as the machining proceeds (we shall deal in more detail with this later). However, on repair work – e.g. truing up a worn shaft and similar – it is desirable to check that the centers match. My own practice, if in doubt, is to use female centers and to fit a hard steel ball between them and the workpiece center.

Given the above precautions, work turned between centers must be round, truly concentric to the axis of rotation, and the work can be turned end for end as often as the need may arise. Provide bearings are in order, the bedways are accurate, and the saddle properly adjusted, it should be possible to turn the full length of a shaft with no detect-

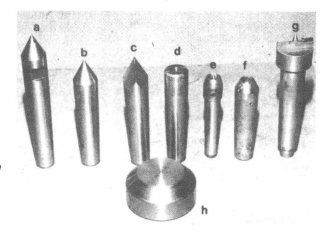

Fig. 6 *Types of center; left to right – a. Hard center, with spanner flats for removal, b. Normal hard or soft center, c. Square center, producing a 60° countersink, d. Female center, e. "Pin and ring" tailstock center for woodturning, f. Hollow tailstock center for wood turning. A drill can be passed through the hole. g. Prong or driver center for wood-turning. h. Home-made pipe center, which fits over the normal cone center.*

Between Centers Work 13

Fig. 7 *Half center in use, facing the end of a bar.*

able difference in diameter along the length.

Types of Centers
The earliest type (so far as metal turning is concerned) was a 90 deg. cone engaged with a punched hole – hence the name 'Center-punch'. If a 60 deg. punch is used this will give satisfactory results on modern centers provided the center itself has no true 'point'; if it has, this will certainly bottom on the punched hole. The SQUARE center, still listed in catalogues, was used as a crude cutter to form a deeper center once the punched one was established in the correct position. I still use it. It saves a lot of fuss trying to center-drill awkward objects! Those sold today produce a proper 60 deg. hole. The FEMALE center is used for workpieces which have a male point on the end (and with steel balls, as mentioned earlier). This applies mainly to watch and clock work, where spindles tend to have pointed pivots. Its limitation is that it is not easy to ensure accuracy of the hole and a worn center cannot be rectified without a great deal of trouble. The HALF-CENTER, (Fig. 7) is used to enable the end of a shaft to be faced while still between centers. The flat does not go to the center of the point, so that at the last there is still a small support to the work. The PIPE CENTER is, as its name implies, a large cone, usually at 90 deg., to engage within large hollow workpieces. A useful variant has a slot down one side, thus enabling the end of a pipe to be machined completely. However, it is an awkward device to use, as the tailstock barrel must be advanced as metal is machined away from the point of contact between work and center.

REVOLVING CENTERS (sometimes called 'running centers') are arranged so that the center itself revolves with the work – it becomes a 'live center'. The cone is supported on a more or less sophisticated bearing system from the part which fits into the tailstock. Their advantage is that they need less adjustment than the normal center, and will withstand greater end-loads. Time is saved in readjustment and they need no lubrication. However, they do put more stress into the workpiece with consequent risk of distortion. They are

Fig. 8 *Jacobs No. 100 "Center-chuck". The end of this dynamo shaft has been damaged, but the commutator still can be turned true.*

bulkier and can get in the way of the topslide at times. Most important – it *is* a live center and as has already been pointed out it will cause eccentricity if it is not absolutely true; there is now a possible source of error at both head- and tailstock ends. Those made by reputable firms will be found to be very accurate, if not perfect, but it must be remembered that if, for any reason, the center does go out of truth it is almost impossible to correct; the part must be replaced.

Finally, a centering device which is seldom seen – I am not even sure of its proper name – I call it a CHUCK-ING CENTER. Fig. 8. This looks like a drill-chuck but the 'jaws' are made of bronze. It is used to support shafts which have damaged centers or no center at all. (The classic case is the lawnmower rotor). Naturally, the other end of the work must be held in the three- or four-jaw chuck, as even if it has a usable center the work must be constrained endways. That shown in the photo is by the Jacobs Company (their No. 100) and accepts work from ¼ in. up to ¾ in. The jaws are adjusted to a close slide fit on the shaft and can then be locked.

Centering the Workpiece

When starting from the rough bar exact centering is not (as a rule) essential, as the part is to be machined, but reasonable truth saves unpleasant machining of an eccentric object as well as avoiding out-of-balance running. Old books always gave a number of methods of marking out the end of the shaft – see Fig. 9. Most of these are self-explanatory, but note that it is *not* necessary to adjust the scriber or dividers to strike the exact center. The crossed lines form a little enclosure and the eye is so precise a measuring instrument that no difficulty is found in setting the point of the center-punch fairly accurately. Once the center found is lightly punched the work is set in the lathe and checked for truth. Any adjustment can then be made by 'drawing' the punched hole. Not, however, as recommended in some books, by knocking the workpiece with a mallet! This is certain to damage the centers. The punch-hole is then deepened and if a 60 deg. punch is used this may well suffice for light work or where extreme accuracy is not needed. Otherwise, a hole is first drilled, either with

Between Centers Work 15

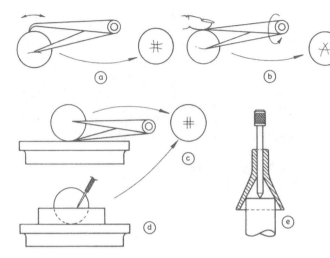

Fig. 9 *Centering methods, a. Jenny calipers, b. Dividers, c. Dividers and flat plate, d. Metal strip, about half the work diameter, and scriber. e. Bell center-punch.*

the hand-drill or in the machine, using a short 3/32 in. drill followed by a 60 deg. countersink cutter. Alternatively, the work may be set in the lathe and each end in turn treated with a combination center-drill held in the tailstock drill-chuck.

There are some special tools for centering the ends of round bars. Of these the BELL CENTER-PUNCH – Fig. 9e – is the simplest to use and is cheap, or can be made. The bell must, of course, be upright in use or the punch will be off-center. The VEE-SQUARE (Fig. 10) is, of course, part of the normal Combination Square outfit (that shown in the photo is a small one). It is hardly worth buying one specially for this job, but centering is easily done if you have one already. Special, similar, devices were sold solely for bar centering at one time but are seldom seen nowadays. Industrial shops where a lot of center-lathe work is done will have installed special bar-centering machines instead.

Fig. 10 *Centering with a Vee-square.*

16 WORKHOLDING IN THE LATHE FOR HOME MACHINISTS

Fig. 11 *Bar set up on vee-blocks, centered using a scribing block.*

Fig. 11 shows a bar being centered using vee-blocks and a marking-out gauge or scribing block. This is an elaboration of method 9d and is as quick a way as any if the tools are to hand. Small bar stock can, of course, be centered on the lathe itself if it has a hollow mandrel and the work will pass through. Held in the three- or four-jaw chuck, a combination center-drill is applied from the tailstock. Indeed, work of any shape may be so treated if it is first set up at the headstock end – a matter which will be dealt with when we come to consider chuck-work. Large stock, which will not pass through, can also be centered from the tailstock by using the FIXED STEADY REST – Fig. 12.

This needs care in setting up – the bar must be truly co-axial with the lathe centers or the drill will be broken. I shall have more to say about this matter when we come to deal with the steady rest in general.

Size of Center Hole
As I have said, the odd job can be machined with no more than a punched center, but a properly proportioned well-fitting center is essential for accurate work. The size of the center must be proportioned both to the size of the work and the depth of cut expected. While a small center *can* support large jobs, and there are cases where a

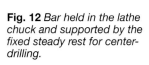

Fig. 12 *Bar held in the lathe chuck and supported by the fixed steady rest for center-drilling.*

Between Centers Work 17

deep hole cannot be accepted, this does need more attention to lubrication and greater risk of scoring or seizure at the tailstock. The heaviest load comes on the hard center when machining at that end, and if most of the cutting will be done at the headstock end then a smaller center hole can safely be used. With careful attention to lubrication, a ¼ in. outside diameter center will withstand the forces involved in taking a full roughing cut on a 3½ in. lathe – say 5/16 in. cut at 0.004 in./rev. in steel. However, I tend to proportion the center to the work diameter, and checking up find that the drill diameter is equal to 3/32 in. + 15% of the work diameter! Thank goodness it is not that critical! It is, of course, important that the combination center-drill is properly depthed – see Fig. 13. If location only is required, then even a 1/16 in. dia. center will serve. Fig. 13a shows a fair range of sizes. The dimensions are the overall diameters.

Unusual Centers
I have already referred to the use of a steel ball and a female center. This had to be used when I was restoring a 17th century church clock, as every arbor seemed to have a different shaped hole in it. But since then I have come across an electric motor with hemispherical centers to the spindle – no doubt there was some production reason for this. Some early machinery has been found with pointed ends to spindles, needing the use of the female center. Wooden objects may be found with what appears to be a point within a ring on the end; this is from the use of the CUP CENTER, Fig. 6e. Returning can safely be done using a normal center instead.

Steady Rests
I shall be dealing with these in detail later on, but will mention just a few points now so far as they relate to work between centers. The main object is to provide support to slender work, where the tool forces might otherwise produce bowing. The emphasis is on the word 'support' and the principles mentioned earlier must be kept in mind. If the steady shoes exert any pressure when the work is running free, then bowing will be inevitable, and this side pressure is inevitable, if the points of the steady shoes are not concentric with the line between centers. This applies both to fixed and traveling steady rests. I use two methods. First, by setting a dial indicator against the workpiece, to read zero without the steady rest, and then

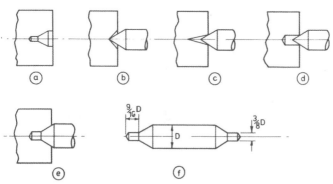

Fig. 13 a. Center too deep. b. Very bad center mismatch, c. Mismatch which is tolerable, d. Plain drilled center – acceptable for light work. e. Optimum depth of center-drilling. f. Approximate proportions of combination centeredrills. ("Slocombe drills")

adjusting this so that the indicator still reads zero. To make sure that the steady is actually bearing, a trace of marking blue is used. The second method, applicable to the fixed steady only, is to release the tailstock center and then check that, with the steady rest engaged, the center-hole is coaxial with the center itself. There are other methods – my only purpose at this stage is to emphasize that great care is needed on this matter.

The traveling steady rest is used mainly when screw-cutting long shafts and here a second point needs attention. If the shoes are of brass or soft material there is a risk that these will become grooved by the embryo thread. If this happens it will be found that the saddle continues to traverse even after the half-nuts are disengaged; embarrassing! Hard steel or cast iron shoes are better for this type of work.

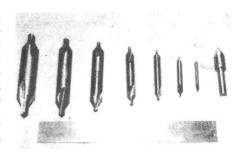

Fig. 13A *A set of Slocombe drills from ⅛ in. to ½ in. dia, with a 60° centering cutter on the right.*

Driving the Work

The soft center in the headstock is incapable of driving the work, and it is usual to fit a DRIVER PLATE or CATCH-PLATE to the mandrel nose, engaging with a CARRIER clipped to the end of the work. Fig. 14 shows a number of

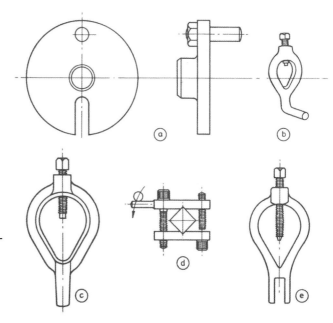

Fig. 14 *a. Driver or catch-plate. b. Bent form of work-carrier or dog. c. Straight carrier. d. Clamp carrier for square or similar work. e. Forked carrier.*

Between Centers Work

Fig. 15 *A collection of carriers or driving dogs. a. Malleable iron. b. Hot-pressed brass c. Forged steel and machined. d. A very small, but not the smallest, size! e. Forked carrier, f. A small example of the clamp type. g. Ring carrier. This dates from 1805, and all the screws seen were turned between centers.*

types. The driver, (a), is provided both with a peg and a slot; in more convenient designs there are several holes so that pegs of different sizes can be fitted at various radii of action. It is a first principle that both peg and carrier be as small as possible, as these parts become almost invisible in work and can cause serious injuries. (All my carriers and pegs are painted bright orange), (b) shows the classical bent carrier, which engages in the slot, but it is to be recommended only on relatively heavy items, as the carrier will exert a bending force on the workpiece as well as driving it round and, especially if there is an interrupted cut, can cause trouble. The straight carrier, (c) comes in many forms – forged, malleable castings, or cut from plate, but all follow the same principle. (Fig. 15 shows a few examples). Those used for – or on – finished work may be of brass or bronze. Even so, it is desirable to use soft packing between the screw and the work. The screw must have a tight grip when roughing and a flat on the work helps. It is good practice to tie the carrier to the catchplate peg, too.

Fig. 14d shows a CLAMP carrier, often made to suit the work, and at 14e is the forked type, where the peg engages between the arms. This is the preferred type of carrier, and some variant is always used on precision grinding machines. Finally, the RING carrier,

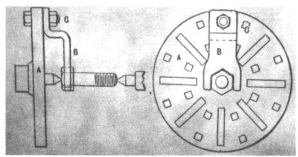

Fig. 16 *100 years ago; a carrier driving a bolt for screwcutting!*

Fig. 17 *These two examples would be regarded as normal "between centers" jobs in the 1880s. In (a) the shaded bosses are used to take the centers, and filed off afterwards. In (b) a loose piece is clamped on to take the tailstock center while turning the upper part of the chair-leg.*

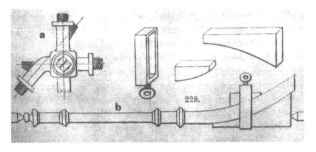

seldom seen nowadays, is shown in the photo Fig. 15g. It has the virtue of being far better balanced than others, and is less hazardous. It can easily be made, and a single carrier will do for a fair range of work diameter. Finally, Fig. 16 shows a method described in an old book for driving hexagon bolts. I make no excuse for drawing examples from these old books, by the way, for the methods used then are often far more applicable to our work than are those of current Production Engineering practice! Many readers, of course, would catch the head of the bolt in the three-jaw chuck, but this device was not in general use until late in the development of the lathe. (Besides, at current prices many beginners may find the cost of a three-jaw more than they can face!) ALL the screws, even tiny ones no more than $3/16$ in. dia., on my Holtzapffel lathe of 1805 were turned between centers.

Non-circular Shapes

This includes eccentrics, crankshafts and so on, for though the *parts* may be circular the parts do not revolve around identical axes. To illustrate my point I show Fig. 17, again from an old book on turning written in 1881. Faced with either of these jobs most present day turners would have to scratch their heads a bit, but 100 years ago they were taken as a matter of course. Today the 4-way cock would probably be turned from a chuck, using chucking-pieces in place of center-bosses, but I have included it 'to give you some ideas'!

The CRANKSHAFT is probably the most common 'eccentric' turning met

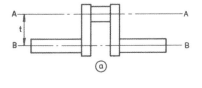

Fig. 18
Supporting a crankshaft while turning the mainshaft or journals.

Between Centers Work 21

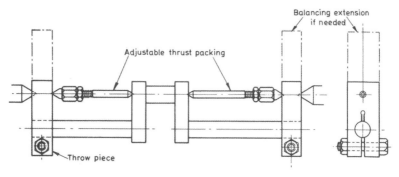

Fig. 19 *Machining the crankpin. See also Fig. 20.*

with by model engineers. I do not propose to deal with the actual machining, but only with its 'support', and will, at this stage, confine my attention to between-centers work. Fig. 18a shows the fundamentals of the problem. We have two axes, AA and BB, separated by a distance equal to the throw, 't'. Axis BB appears to present few problems; we can simply center the ends and turn the shaft in the normal way. However, if we do this the end-pressure from the tailstock will distort the shaft. We must apply thrust packing as shown in Fig. 18b. This must just fit – no more and no less. If too tight it will spread the webs outwards; if slack, the center-pressure will not be relieved. (Not only the center-pressure, either, for in machining there will be tool-forces as well.) So, the best practice is first to do some preliminary work, filing smooth the inner face and sides of the webs. The packing can then be fitted properly, and I always advise fitting a clamp also – Fig. 18c. This not only retains the packing, but also stiffens up the weakest part of the system.

To machine the crankpin AA some means of offset centering is needed, and this is usually provided by THROWPIECES, Fig. 19. It is, of course, important that the offset on each throwpiece is the same, and my own practice is to use 'Co-ordinate setting' to ensure accuracy. The throwpiece is set up on the vertical slide and the centers spaced using the cross-slide index as a micrometer. The center hole can be cut with a Slocombe drill, and the hole for the shaft either drilled and reamed or, preferably, bored with an offset boring head from the headstock. Though the two throwpieces are made separately they will, if care has been taken to allow for backlash in the feedscrew nut, be identical. The throwpieces must also be accurately aligned but that is beyond the scope of this book. We need thrust packing here again and this time there are two, both being adjustable. Note the pointed ends, which engage in small centerpops in both throwpiece and web, to prevent them from coming adrift. For larger shafts it pays to extend the throwpieces, as shown dotted, to provide some small degree of balance and so enable a higher cutting speed when finishing the crankpin.

My procedure for such shafts is first to rough out the webs by milling or filing. Then machine the journals almost to size with just sufficient to

Fig. 20 *In this case the thrust pieces are toolmaker's jacks. The shaft is ½-inch diameter.*

exact size at each end to fit the throwpieces. Any machining needed on the webs is also done to within a few mil of dimension. The throwpieces and jacks are then fitted and the crankpin and associated web flanks are brought to finish size. Finally, the journals and webs are machined to final size – with the center thrust piece and clamp still in place. This procedure ensures that any slight distortion which may occur (especially with a heavy forged steel shaft or, worse, one chewed from BDMS) can be corrected in the finishing cuts on the mainshaft. See Fig. 20.

For multi-throw shafts the need for careful packing is even more important – they are slender enough as it is. The

Fig. 21 *Throwpieces for a three-throw crankshaft. Note the scribed and punched lines, used in the initial setting up.*

throwpieces need some consideration also. You can use single ones as shown in Fig. 19 and readjust them for each crank, but I prefer to use circular discs of some thickness with all three centers

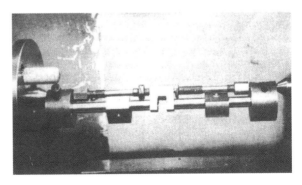

Fig. 22 *Set-up for machining the center crankpin. In this case the slots between the webs were milled out just before each crankpin was turned.*

Between Centers Work 23

Fig. 23 Web clamps and thrust packing for the shaft shown in Fig. 22. The threaded jack-screws had to be reduced locally to clear adjacent webs.

cut on each. This means that once right for one throw they will be correct for all. Figs. 21 and 22 show such a pair. These were drilled by co-ordinate methods ensuring both proper phasing of the cranks and the correct throw. By the time the final, finishing, cut is made on the journals the shaft as a whole is very flexible. As well as using clamps on the webs the use of a steady rest is almost imperative. Work from the tailstock end, so that the 'drive' section of the shaft is as stiff as possible, and fit the steady rest to the journal nearest to the saddle, being moved to the next one when machining the intermediate journal. Then turn the shaft end-for-end and repeat the process. Fig. 23 shows the thrustpieces and the web clamps used in machining such a shaft.

The machining of ECCENTRICS on a solid shaft – a rare occurrence – can be done in a similar manner, though there is no need for web packing and seldom for thrust rods. In the case of eccentrics the phase angle is very important indeed. The throw can be set out with reasonable accuracy by co-ordinate methods but though the co-ordinates can be accurately *determined* for the angles, the slides (especially the vertical slide) cannot be set to the tenths of mils required. For this reason those who have a dividing head will find that it pays to set this up for the purpose. The throw is set using the cross slide index, and the relative angles determined using the division plate. If the same throwpiece is used both for the crank throws and for the eccentrics, then accuracy of phasing between cranks and eccentrics is assured. It is a fairly time-consuming set-up, but the only way to establish correct valve-timing when the eccentrics are not adjustable.

Taper Turning

As has already been pointed out, if the tailstock is not disposed truly axial to the lathe center the workpiece will be turned taper. This is put to use when we *need* a taper shaft. The tailstock is set over, towards the operator if the tail end is to be smaller and vice versa, the amount of the offset being half the required diametral taper. Thus if a taper of $1/8$ in. per foot is required on work 6 in. long, the tailstock must be set over by $1/32$ inch. This offset must be checked with a dial indicator or similar means, and it is important to check this with the tailstock locked to the bed, as the locking device may cause very slight movement. An important point is that the offset must be calculated on the *actual* length of the workpiece, including any waste which may be turned or parted off from the ends later.

The trouble of altering the tailstock and subsequently resetting to turn parallel may be avoided by using an OFFSET CENTER. These can be made or purchased, but whose who own a boring head with a taper shank which fits the tailstock socket can make use of this instead. This requires no more than the manufacture of a hard center to fit in place of the normal boring tool. Fig. 24 shows my own – the well known ABC boring head. It use makes things a great deal easier. Not only is there no need to alter the tailstock, but the head itself is calibrated in thousandths so that the 'first trial' offset is usually the last. It is, of course, necessary to establish that the zero on the boring head scale does, in fact, bring the center point truly central. My own has a zero error of about 0.003 in., a fact which is noted on the box.

The offset center method cannot be used for steep tapers, for if the offset is too great the center will not engage properly – Fig. 25. This shows the effect exaggerated, but it will be noticed that the center bears on the outer end of the hole on one side and on the inner at the other. The hole will wear to a more or less curved shape in time, and readjustment of the center will be required frequently at first. If the taper is a steep one (the

Fig. 24 *An offset boring head can be used as a set-over tailstock center for taper turning.*

actual offset depends, of course, on the length of the workpiece) then it is inadvisable to use the offset method and either the topslide must be set over and the taper 'picked up' if its travel is not long enough, or a taper-turning attachment must be used. In passing, Fig. 25 shows that it is desirable, where possible, for the tailstock to be set over *away* from the operator, thus ensuring that tool thrust is taken on the large diameter of the center-hole.

Mandrels

A mandrel is a device whereby bored workpieces can be turned between centers. They are taper, about 0.0005 in./inch, as opposed to an ARBOR, which is a similar but parallel device. Commercial mandrels are hardened, usually right through in sizes below an inch or so, larger ones being casehardened and ground. The small end is usually about one mil below the

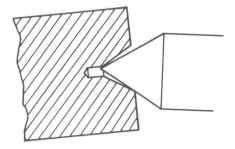

Fig. 25 *Effect of attempting to turn too steep a taper by tailstock offset. The same geometry will apply to the headstock center also.*

nominal diameter, but this does vary. Homemade mandrels can be finish turned and polished – hardening is not essential and can, indeed, be a disadvantage at times; though the mandrel may be damaged if the tool cuts into it this is often less serious than rubbing off the point of the tool, and making a new mandrel when the old one is scored beyond further use is no great matter.

In use the mandrel is slightly oiled and the work pressed or 'jarred' onto it by bumping the large end onto a piece of lead or wood. Great force should not be used, but there must be sufficient grip to prevent the work from turning on the mandrel. This is very much a matter of judgement and no rule can be laid down. The whole is then set between centers, in such a way that the tool forces will be towards *the larger end*, for obvious reasons. The work may now be treated like any other 'between centers' operation, except that cuts may have to be lighter than usual. First because the grip of the work on the mandrel is limited, and second, because the mandrel itself presents a relatively slender section of the assembly and if care is not taken chatter may occur. Tools should always be especially sharp.

The EXPANDING, or adjustable, mandrel is a very useful piece of equipment, as it can be used on nonstandard diameter holes – when work is part machined, for example. They come

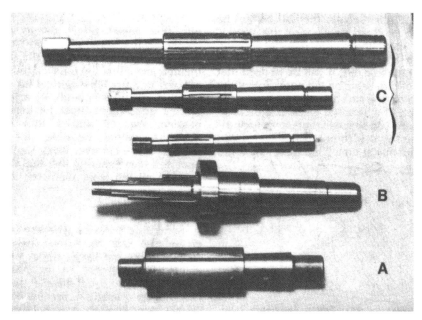

Fig. 26 *Adjustable mandrels, a. Split cast-iron sleeve on a taper mandrel by Birch, b. The "LeCount" type. c. Three sizes of adjustable mandrel which will cover from 0.36 inch to 1.05 inch between them.*

in many forms and Fig. 26 shows three types. That marked 'A' is a very early type by BIRCH & CO., comprising a split cast iron sleeve fitting on a taper arbor. The amount of adjustment on each sleeve is small, (several are provided) and in industrial use the sleeve would be machined to suit the work in hand, mounted on the arbor. It is robust and will stand fairly heavy cuts. The center example, 'B', by the C.W. LeCount Corp., U.S.A., has three stepped members sliding in grooves with a taper base. The work is butted up to the shoulder and then jarred home on the taper. The range is large and the grip from the relatively narrow members is good. However, in time these sliding parts get worn, and accuracy suffers. (They can, of course, be remachined). Above is a set of unknown make covering the range from just below ⅜ in. to just over 1 in. diameter. The sliding sleeve and the arbor are both of hardened and ground steel, the former being in the form of a concertina-like spring. They are surprisingly accurate and give a good grip, but the tool thrust *must* be towards the larger end of the taper.

There are many other forms of SPECIAL MANDRELS, including those on which an accurate thread is screwcut, so that work can be screwed on up to a shoulder; parallel mandrels or arbors with a threaded end and locknut and even square or polygonal ones, on which work is either secured with turner's ce-ment or held with a locknut on a threaded end. All have the same object – to enable work which might otherwise have to be chucked to be turned between centers, with all the advantages that gives. The major limitation has already been mentioned; the arbor presents a relatively slender support and due allowance must be made for this fact.

Between Centers – Conclusion

There is one aspect of work between centers on which I have not touched – the case where the work is held in a chuck at the headstock end, but on a center at the tailstock. This was very common in the 19th century, when round or square cup-chucks were used to drive the work, which was just roughly shaped and hammered into the cup. It is legitimate to support one end of long work, but using the three- or four-jaw chuck, and I shall be dealing with this when we come to chuck work.

To sum up, provided the centers are correctly shaped and truly aligned (and all else is in order) between-centers turning produces the most accurate and most repeatable of all methods, even when the workpiece is so short that it could readily be chuck held. Further, it is possible to contrive to hold the most unlikely objects between centers. The three-jaw self-centering chuck is by no means an *essential* accessory; a set of hard and soft centers most certainly is.

CHAPTER 2

Faceplate Work

Very early in the history of the lathe it was realized that the machine could be used to face across objects of large diameter as well as turning between centers. 'Facing Chucks' consisting of discs drilled with many holes or, as seen in Fig. 27, tapped to receive screws, were 'optional equipment' to most lathes, to be screwed onto the mandrel nose. In the watch and clock-making industry a special lathe known as the 'Mandrel' was a standard machine designed solely for facing and drilling clock plates or large wheels, and early in the 19th century 'facing and boring' lathes of very large size were built, again with no provision for work of any great lengths and having no tailstock. The perforated faceplate, often with more holes than plate, gave way to the slotted type with which we are familiar – not always an advantage – and Fig. 28 shows some from my own machines. Two are from the Myford, the smaller one being that supplied as standard equipment. Above these can

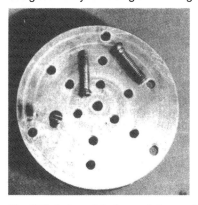

Fig. 27 *left, faceplate from a lathe made in 1805. The screws have deep rectangular threads, and all have been screwcut.* **Fig. 28** *right, a group of faceplates. Note the setting rings. (See text).*

28 WORKHOLDING IN THE LATHE FOR HOME MACHINISTS

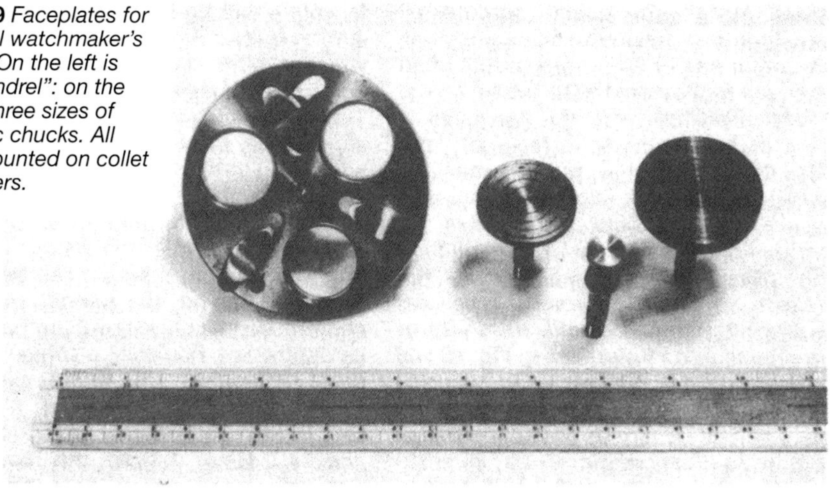

Fig. 29 *Faceplates for a small watchmaker's lathe. On the left is a "Mandrel": on the right three sizes of shellac chucks. All are mounted on collet adapters.*

be seen what looks like a chuck backplate but is, in fact, one to which thin work is attached by soldering or 'Turner's Cement'. Alongside is a 'Mandrel' from my Lorch, with a set of three special clips holding a thin disc for a boring operation. Further types are seen in Fig. 29, from a small Boley watchmaker's lathe; the small ones are wax or cement chucks, while on the left is a true 'Watchmaker's Mandrel' similar to that in Fig. 28, but fitted with a 'pump center'. With such a wide variety of holding devices the turner must consider very carefully which to use and, more important, how to use it. For, while the faceplate was first introduced for plain facing work, its advantages for other classes of turning were soon realized.

First, an important point about the facing operation itself. We are accustomed to think of the faceplate as being 'flat', but this is not the case. All machines are subject to some degree of error, and even if perfect when new will suffer from wear in due course. A little reflection will show that if there *is* to be an error it is better for this to be such that the surface will be faced *concave* rather than convex, so that two mating surfaces will not rock when fitted to each other. The headstock/cross slide alignment is, therefore, always set up so that this feature is built into the machine. The concavity will be very

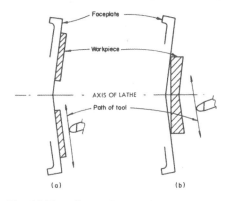

Fig. 30 *The effects of concavity. (a) Workpieces set around the rim of the faceplate. (b) Across the centers.*

Faceplate Work   29

small; on a good quality commercial machine the maximum allowance will be about one or two thousandths of an inch per foot of tool travel, while on my Lorch precision lathe the concavity is less than 8 tenths foot. Naturally, the less this is the better, but any machine which showed the slightest amount of *convex* error would be rejected on inspection, and sent back for rebuilding. (In passing, this 'concavity' is the reason why large diameter flycutters suffer interference on the back half of the revolution.) Reference to Fig. 30 will reveal that if a number of workpieces are set around the faceplate as at (a) they will all be turned sensibly parallel, but any set across the center, as at (b) will be concave. On my 9 inch faceplate the concavity amounts to less than ¾ of a mil over the full diameter.

Holding the Work
Reference back to the first chapter will show that it is not possible to hold a workpiece to a faceplate using the 'no grip' technique. If we are to have but one degree of freedom (in rotation) then the stops needed to effect restraint will lie in the way of the tool. We must, therefore, rely on *clamping,* and the implications of this must now be considered. In effect, a clamp is a device which applies so much force that the friction between (e.g.) the work and the faceplate will be much larger than the cutting forces. As we shall see later, we can combine clamps and stops, but some form of clamping will be required. The important point to note is that as soon as any force is applied to the work some distortion is inevitable; you *cannot* apply a force to anything without causing a deflection. In many circumstances this deflection is not important, but in others it can be fatal. In Fig. 31, at (a), the flanges may be compressed a little but the top face will be unaffected. However, a similar workpiece shown at (b) would certainly deflect and, after machining, the top face will almost certainly be found to be convex. How much this matters depends on the nature of the job, but a better arrangement for (b) would be to have forked clamps, gripping at the ends of the bridge section.

The apparently safe condition of Fig. 31 (a) may inadvertently be translated to that of 31 (b) if there is any particle of swarf between the work and the faceplate, or if there is a burr on either workpiece or faceplate. Absolute cleanliness is important, and the faceplate must be examined periodically for dents and burrs. It is good practice to set a piece of paper between machined work and the faceplate, too. This not only reduces the risk from small burrs but, in addition, compensates for any

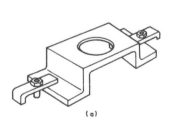

(a)

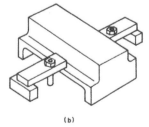

(b)

Fig. 31 (a) Clamps correctly applied, to cause little distortion. (b) Clamping here will distort the top face.

minute irregularities. It also improves the frictional grip. Incidentally, when remachining faceplates (and this is sometimes necessary, and essential when transferring from one machine to another) a dead smooth surface is not required, still less a highly polished one. A 'fine machine finish' will give a better grip.

A second factor must also be kept in mind when machining rough castings or work of an irregular shape. This is the principle of 'three-point support'. No matter how carefully it may be packed it is very difficult indeed for anything with more (or less) than three legs to be supported in a stable manner. That is why surface plates have only three pads underneath. Even if a machined surface is set upon another there is risk of rock (especially if any dirt be there) and any clamping will then cause distortion. When attaching irregular work to the faceplate, therefore, it is important to arrange packing so that the piece is supported at *three points only;* and, bearing in mind what has already been said, three clamps as near to this packing as possible. It is, of course, not always practicable to achieve these ideals, (we may need three pieces of packing but have room for but two clamps) but they should always be kept in mind.

Fig. 32 shows a flywheel attached to the faceplate for remedial work on the bore. It is packed away from the plate to permit the boring tool to pass through without fouling the mandrel nose, but similar packing would have been used in machining a rough casting, so that the tool could traverse across the circumference when machining. The packing positions are marked with chalk The clamps are set across the pairs of spokes

Fig. 32 *A nine-inch flywheel set on the large faceplate of fig. 28 for remedial work on the bore. The chalk-marks indicate the position of the packing – see text.*

adjacent to the packing. It would have been better had the packing been directly under three spoke ends, and the clamps *across* these spokes, but here we run up against a difficulty common to most faceplates. Manufacturers appear to be ignorant of the 'three point' principle and always make the plates with four or eight slots! Twelve would be better, as then there would be the choice, but there it is! With eight slots it just was not possible (on this job) to arrange clamps across the spokes. However, the job is reasonably stiff, and the clamps are as close to the rim as possible. Had the work been slender I should have drilled and tapped the faceplate to suit.

Faceplate Dogs

The problem with clamps is that they tend to project above the work – if they do not, then the bolts may do so. See Fig. 33. The *dog* is a device which enables the work to be clamped laterally, and they are easily made. Fig.

Faceplate Work 31

Fig. 34 *A set of faceplate dogs.*

Fig. 33 *A tricky clamping job – the clamps must be set to clear the tool. The designer has provided packing lugs on the casting in this case, which can be filed to make a secure bed for the work.*

34 shows my set, but if I were making another outfit I would not have the shanks rectangular as seen, but simply a circular stem so that the dog could be rotated in the slot. Fig. 35 shows these dogs in use. They are inside the workpiece, which is not typical, but this frame was the only example I had by me which I could use to illustrate the point. The dogs are in the corners, so that there is no bending stress in the frames and after tightening – not too much – the work is tapped back to the faceplate with a rawhide mallet. These dogs do have other uses, one of which is to act as a stop when the workpiece is such that the cut is interrupted, thus causing a shock load, too fragile to

Fig. 35 *Faceplate dogs in use. Though it might have been possible to set clamps in the slots of the workpiece the bolts would almost certainly have projected and fouled the tool.*

clamp with any force. In circular work they have the advantage that they make the centering operation much easier.

Safety Note for Adhesives

Metalworkers remove materials differently than woodworkers as metals can get hot and alter the bond between the workpiece and fixture. Be careful when using adhesives on metal workpieces (which is often rare and used as a final resort) as the workpiece and process can cause vibrations that can dislodge the workpiece from the adhesion. Note that the examples given in this book are used on small parts with minimal removal required to ensure there is minimal heat and friction introduced to the workpiece.

Attachment with Adhesives

Woodturners are accustomed to gluing work to their faceplates, and it is surprising that more metalworkers do not follow their example. It was very common 100 years ago, but seems to have been lost sight of. I have used the term 'adhesive' but this does include soldering. Fig. 36 shows the loose portface of my beam engine 'MARY' being soldered to a small faceplate. This plate is cast-iron, but has been tinned all over (though it does not show) and the workpiece is being sweated to it. If the work is tinned also, and both work and plate heated together, the thickness of the solder film will tend to equalize naturally and accurate thicknessing can be achieved. Accurate centering is not so easy, as this must be done with the assembly hot. If done on the lathe mandrel there is risk of finding the plate 'shrunk on' when all cools! However, if you have a dummy mandrel nosepiece you can arrange this in a loose bearing in the vice and spin it round, centering the work with a wooden skewer or similar tool. As a rule, however, I seldom solder-fix when accurate centering is needed, preferring the use of glue.

If there is no hurry, then 'Araldite Rapid' is excellent. The tubes should be warmed to about 100 deg. F to reduce the viscosity and the tailstock used to exert slight pressure to squeeze the glue into a uniform thickness. You then have about 3 minutes during which it is possible to ajust the sideways position; the work must then be left to cure. I find half an hour on my storage heater gives adequate strength. The adhesive is brittle, so that a sharp blow with a wooden mallet will detach it. The anaerobic adhesives (Loctite etc) are equally useful, but you must leave them under pressure from the tailstock while curing, as they may slide off.

Turner's Cement is an old – very old – concoction. I have half-a-dozen varieties here, all home made. The strongest is a mixture of powdered pumice stirred into melted shellac, but it is a pig to make; for general purposes a mixture of three parts common resin with one part beeswax – melted together and cast into sticks – serves well, with

Fig. 36 *Portface for a beam-engine cylinder being soldered to the faceplate – actually a spare chuck backplate.*

Fig. 37 *A ring attached to the faceplate with turner's cement – partially machined, with the saddle retracted for clarity.*

Faceplate Work 33

a shear strength of about 200 lb.sq.in. (Do not overheat in the mixing, by the way). This can be used in two ways. If truly centralized work is not needed one just holds the stick on the plain faceplate until friction melts it and gives a good cover; then hold the work against the plate until friction again melts the wax – and let go! As soon as all has cooled the work will be held firmly. For more accurate work the plate is heated and the work may then be accurately centered. Fig. 37. In this case there is less risk of shrinking the plate onto the mandrel, as a temperature of little more than 150 deg. F is needed. Again, the job may be detached with a blow, but warm water will do just as well. In facing a number of rings to thickness these can be set in a circle on the faceplate with this cement; the trick is to have all the rings touching each other round the plate, so that the shock load of the interrupted cut is taken by the rings in series, as it were. I have machined as many as 24 rings at once, 1/32 in. thick, this way, and held a tolerance of ± 0.001 in. See Fig. 37A.

The watchmaker makes much use of plain shellac, on the little 'chucks' (really tiny faceplates) seen in Fig. 29. The technique is the same – either using friction or heating with a spirit lamp, the latter when centering is important. If there is a center-hole, then the rest is brought forward and the work centered with a cocktail stick applied to it, the lathe running slowly till the shellac sets. If there is no center-hole, then a piece of pegwood is applied to the outer circumference. The procedure is quick and very effective. (Fig. 38). In fine work it is important that the thickness of the wax or shellac be uniform, and light pressure should be applied. Resin alone is a substitute for shellac, but rather more brittle.

A final 'adhesive' method is to use double-sided tape – a modern development. I make a great deal of use of this in wood and ivory turning. There are two types of this tape – the very thin material, and a slightly thicker, but somewhat spongy material. The latter is stickier, and will accommodate to rougher surfaces, but naturally

Fig. 37A *A set of washers being thinned. They are attached to the "temporary faceplate" with turner's cement. Each washer touches its neighbor.*

Fig. 38 *Brass ring attached to the faceplate of a watchmaker's lathe with shellac.*

will not be so accurate as it is not so uniform in thickness. The thinner variety is only a few mil thick and very uniform, better for accurate model engineering work. However, a few points must be watched. The concavity I have already mentioned means that the thin material will only grip at the outer part of the work. In fact, this is no disadvantage, as a strip round the edge of the work will hold so firmly that it may be difficult to remove the job! Neither type will adhere to an oily surface and degreasing of both work and faceplate is vital; finger-marks also will reduce the sticking power. It is very strong both in shear and tension (I often have to soak in acetone or denatured alcohol to get the stuff to unstick) but the 'peel' strength is low. On VERY thin work, therefore, light cuts are imperative otherwise the tool may lift the edge. (e.g. if machining 10-mil shimstock down to eight-mil, two cuts would be prudent!) Figs 37 and 38 show machining work this way, the first two with turner's cement, the other with shellac.

Fixtures on the Faceplate

By 'fixture' we mean any device which is attached to the faceplate to hold the work. The most common in early times was the *angle-plate,* and in those days all faceplates had a set of slots specially for this attachment. Fig. 39. (The angle-plate was often part of the outfit). Fig. 40 shows one example of this in use. Here, a cross-drilling jig is being machined. It is important that both the longitudinal hole and the cross-hole be on the centerline exactly. The procedure is to drill and ream the larger bore with the work set on the angle-plate, then rotate the work setting this hole parallel with the faceplate; finally drill and ream the cross-hole. The two are

Fig. 39 *Faceplate of a 20 inch swing Britannia lathe of about 1890. Note the three parallel slots for attaching an angle-plate.*

Fig. 40 *Use of an angle-plate to ensure that two holes are exactly on the same center. Note the offset balance weights.*

Fig. 41 *Setting up a model engine crosshead. After machining the piston-rod hole the work will be rotated to get the crosshead pin hole square, and on the same centerline.*

Faceplate Work   35

then bound to be correct. Fig. 41 shows another application of this same type – in this case the crosshead of a model engine. The angleplate can also be used effectively for cylinder boring and, one end having been faced, can then be set upright to machine the portface and finally the back end cylinder flange can be faced. This was the normal method of boring model cylinders at one time, and very effective too, before all lathes had boring tables.

Fig. 42 *Machining a pump air-vessel connection using a vee-block. This job could not have been held in any other way.*

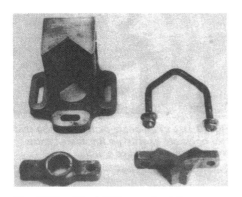

Fig. 43 *The "Keats" Vee-angle plate.*

Vee-blocks are another very useful type of fixture. Fig. 42 shows an awkward workpiece (not a model, but a repair job) which could scarcely have been machined in any other way. Oddly enough I had had this 'double' angle-plate for many years but until this job cropped up never appreciated the usefulness of the twin supports! A specialized form of vee-block is that known as the 'KEATS', shown in Fig. 43, being a combination of angle-plate and vee-block. It has a variety of uses, though it was originally designed for cylinder boring, as in Fig. 44. However, it can be used in many ways, Fig. 45 being set up to show an example. This *is* just an example, for if actually doing the job I would have removed the piston rings first, but I *have* rebored and bushed a gudgeon pin hole this way a fair time ago.

Special *jigs* are frequently well worth while. (The two tapped holes in the small plate in Fig. 28 are for one) Fig. 46 shows an example. Here we have a twin-cylinder block to bore, and the relation of the bores to each other

Fig. 44 *Keats angleplate used when boring an engine cylinder.*

36 WORKHOLDING IN THE LATHE FOR HOME MACHINISTS

Fig. 45 Using the Keats angleplate with the Vee transversely, re-machining the gudgeon-pin hole for a gas engine piston. Note the use of the special clamp giving access to the hole.

Fig. 46 Cylinder boring jig on the faceplate. The jig is hollowed out to receive the boring tool at extreme travel.

Fig. 47 Main bearing boring jig on the faceplate.

and to the holes for the engine columns was important. The jig is arranged so that it can be used first to drill the column holes. It is then set on the faceplate with these in correct relationship to the first cylinder center; when this is bored the casting is reversed on the jig and the second cylinder is bored. As the same jig is used to drill the column holes in the bed *and* to set out the main bearing centers the final alignment of the engine was straightforward.

Fig. 47 shows another jig. Two triple expansion engines were needed for a twin-screw boat. This involved the boring of 8 main bearings, and this could not be done by 'line boring' in place on the bed – the best method. The brasses (actually gunmetal) were made of two pieces soldered together in the usual way, and machined all over externally. The jig was then made as seen in the photo and carefully centered on the faceplate. The pairs of brasses were dropped into the rectangular slot and held by the top clamp. They were then bored and sized with a reamer in the usual way. As all the slots in the beds had been milled at one setting the holes were bound to be accurately aligned and, in this case, it was found that the brasses were interchangeable to the test mandrel.

As a final example, Fig. 48 shows a locomotive driver being turned on the rim. The usual practice of machining the back and boring for the axle is followed, this work being done in the four-jaw

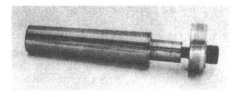

Fig. 48 *Machining a model locomotive driver, with a Morse taper stub mandrel spigot in the mandrel bore, shown above, to ensure concentricity. (Photo – Martin Evans)*

chuck. A fixture comprising a No. 2 Morse taper plug with a peg a push fit to the wheel bore is fitted in the mandrel (with a drawbar, please!) and the wheel is then held to this with a nut on the spigot. Normally, friction will give sufficient drive to the wheel, but I prefer to fit a small driver peg between a couple of the spokes. The great virtue of this method is that the mass of the faceplate acts as a very efficient damper and prevents chatter. (I must add that it is nearly 35 years since I machined a large locomotive driver, and I am indebted to Martin Evans for the photo!)

Temporary Faceplates
I have in the past, frequently made reference to what is almost the best friend the machinist has – the 'block of wood'. All the faceplates on my main Holtzapffel lathe are of wood, some with a metal insert to fit the mandrel nose. They have the great advantage that I can machine right into them if need be, and they can be turned with spigots, recesses, or whatever is needed to accommodate the work in hand. I use the same device on both the Myford and the Lorch, but attach a blank of wood to the standard metal faceplate from behind. I can then machine right into the temporary face with no damage. More important, if I have a workpiece which has just a single projection on the back face which makes holding awkward I can carve out a cavity to receive this and then clamp or screw the work to the wood. The material is not critical – I have used everything from a piece of old scaffold-plank to a chunk of lignum vitae. If using a softwood, however, it is important to get it dry first, and to try to get whatever job is in hand completed in the one day. Softwood can move a lot with changes in humidity.

Centering Work
We shall have more to say about this when we come to chuckwork, but a few words now will not be out of place. With rough castings such as flywheels and the like the initial setting can be done on the bench using the setting rings on the faceplate. After fitting on the lathe the use of chalk and slow rotation enables the work to be set to about 1/64 in.; closer if a felt pen is used instead. However, the error made by many is to set such a wheel to the outside of the casting. The best place to set true to is the *inside* of the rim – i.e. to an unmachined part, which will show when the model is finished. In some cases it is necessary to effect a compromise between truth of the inner

rim and that of the boss, but in general an out-of-true boss is less important. Once reasonably true the slide-rest can be used; advance the cross slide till the tool just touches, then rotate the work half a revolution and repeat. If the index reading is noted at each trial the amount by which the work must be moved can be estimated. If the work is still only lightly clamped and a 'blunt instrument' used instead of a tool the work can be eased over by using the cross slide hand-wheel, but I prefer to use a light rawhide or plastic mallet. Note that the work will often move sideways as well as in the desired direction – one of the clauses of that famous law! There is no point in attempting to get the work running closer than the roughness of the casting. If centering to a previously drilled hole is needed, then it will usually suffice to bring up the tailstock center to the hole, but if a *bored* hole is to be picked up, then a dial indicator must be used.

For setting previously machined work on the faceplate the normal dial indicator method is used, (Fig. 49) though I always precede this by using the cross slide index as previously described. For much work this will be sufficient in itself – I find I can set to two or three mil runout this way. But do not use a sharp pointed tool as the 'sensor' as this will dig into the surface, not only giving a false reading but also leaving marks on the job. For setting to a marked center, of course, the old established 'center-finder' or 'wobbler' is standard practice.

Whatever the nature of the workpiece it is important that a check be made after the final tightening of any clamps. These need seldom be so tight that a dull blow with a lead hammer

Fig. 49 *Setting central to a machined bore. The cylinder is due to be faced at the end and then counterbored. Note the use of three clamps only.*

cannot shift the work. Most people clamp up far too tightly, and it is only when there will be a vicious interrupted cut that really tight clamps are needed. Indeed, I prefer, in such cases, to use my normal clamping pressure, but add a stop peg (one of my faceplate dogs as a rule) to take the shock thrust.

It is sometimes necessary to set work true to the face – i.e. across the bed – by adjustment of packing behind the work. This is a tedious business, the more so as the packing always falls out at the critical moment! Large packing pieces can be induced to stay put by magnetizing them, but an equally effective expedient is to coat them with Evo-stik or one of the other similar glues. I have some stuff called 'Cow Gum' which works well provided there is no oil about.

Adjustment in this plane can be done using the slide index method, but with the topslide index or the leadscrew hand-wheel as the indicator.

Faceplate Work 39

Precautions

Work running above about 150 r.p.m. must be balanced. If the workpiece is at all weighty and we are (say) boring a small hole therein at the proper speed, then the out-of-balance forces will not only rock the machine on its bench, but also put a hefty load on the mandrel bearings. These have an oil clearance, and the out of balance can easily lead to dimensional errors. In a number of the photos you will see odd weights attached to serve this end. Total accuracy is not essential, but if the machine shows any signs of vibration, look to this point. (Not forgetting that too much balance weight is as bad as too little!)

Inevitably in faceplate work there will be bolts, lugs, dogs, and the aforesaid weights projecting. All too often these foul the gap in the bed! Or they may foul the toolholder. So, check by hand rotation that everything will clear with the saddle in the extreme working position. Worse, however, is the risk that these projections may foul *you,* and you will finish with a visit to the casualty ward. It may break your heart to do so, but it is best to saw off any excess projection of bolts – better saw *them* off than have the vet saw off a finger. I try to paint all such hazards with yellow cellulose, so that there is a visual warning.

A final point; the faceplate is, when new, an accurately-machined accessory. Take care to keep it so, for burrs will spoil it. I have already referred to the need to remachine if transferred from one lathe to another (I have had my 9 in. Myford for nearly 40 years, on three lathes) and though not likely it MAY be necessary to remachine a new plate after a year or so if the original casting missed the aging process. If machining up a casting for a replacement, rough it out and leave it for as long as you can before taking the finishing cut. Now, just think a little. When you *do* take the finishing cut, this is the one which determines the final accuracy. If you use the classic 'two mil per rev' and a shaving depth of cut, the tool is going to run about 800 yards during the process, and an interrupted cut across the slots at that, and some slight wear is inevitable. So much so that if the cut is only a mil or so you may well find it stops cutting altogether when part way across. The trick is to use a somewhat coarser feed – I would suggest 6 to 8 mil/rev, or even ten mil – a very sharp tool with a fairly large radius at the cutting edge, and a cut sufficiently deep to prevent any risk of rubbing; not less than three mil. Work from the inside outwards, so that any tool wear produces concavity – the reverse traverse could make it convex. Then, when finished, use a pointed tool to cut a number of concentric circles at, say, half-inch intervals, to help in rough centering. For some reason lathe manufacturers never do this, and it is always the first machining job one has to do on a new lathe after the initial setting up.

CHAPTER 3

Chuckwork – General

In earlier days the word 'chuck' was used to describe anything that drove the work. What we call a 'catchplate', for example, was known as a 'driver chuck'. Their names were legion; J. J. Holtzapffel takes 64 pages to describe them in his book on 'Plain Turning', and he did not include all the 'Ornamental' types. I myself have over two dozen different *sorts* of chucks, ranging from plain wooden blocks to very complex devices indeed. All have their uses, and I will deal with some which have a general application to model engineering in a later section. However, let us first look at those which we should recognize as chucks in this day and age.

The main characteristic is that the chuck 'grips'. The work is held between jaws or screws (or both). The simplest type is the screw bell chuck (Fig. 50) comprising a metal cup with screws – usually eight but sometimes four – passing through the wall to hold the workpiece. A device not to be disdained, as experienced users of both watchmaker's lathes and the old ADEPT lathe will know. We will have a look at this one later. Most readers, however, will know only those with three or four jaws, working in slides machined in a substantial body, and operated by screws or a scroll engaging with the back of the jaw. All

Fig. 50 *left;* A 4-screw bell chuck dating from 1805. *right;* A modern 8-screw bell chuck.

Fig. 51 *Checking the effect of jaw pressure on a ring.*

exert sufficient pressure to overcome the reactions from the cutting tool. There is absolutely *no* way in which the work can resist the jaw pressure without distortion, for that is one of nature's laws. And, by the same token, no way in which the chuck can exert this force without itself suffering some degree of distortion, too. As we shall see later, this is most unfortunate, as in the most commonly used type – the self-centering three-jaw chuck – this distortion occurs just in that element upon which we rely for its accuracy.

In Fig. 51 I show a ring, of 5/16 in. square cross-section, held in a self-centering chuck. It has been 'reasonably' gripped and then bored true. A dial test indicator applied to the inside of the ring showed negligible deflection. The jaws were then tightened in a 'casual' fashion – just a twist with one hand, with no excessive force. The dial indicator then showed the ring to be 'lobed', having sprung inwards in way of the jaws and outwards in between them. The total runout was then about 0.005 inch. Fig. 52 shows another case. Here we have a substantial flywheel, previously machined on the faceplate, so that we can assume that the rim is true. It has been set in the four-jaw independent chuck and centered, using just sufficient force to hold it. The d.t.i. showed a very small deflection – a total runout of about 0.0005 inch. The jaws were then carefully tightened to provide a grip which I would have considered proper for rough machining the casting. The dial now showed a lobed runout of about 3 mil – and this despite the fact that the chuck jaws are adjacent to the spokes. This rim is ¾ in. wide and ½ in. radial thickness, with spokes averaging ⅜ in. diameter. There has been some distortion nevertheless and it would,

too often miscalled solely by the number of jaws, an error which can sometimes lead to confusion!

First, let us get down to a few basic principles. All these devices *grip*. An immediate consequence is that the workpiece has lost all the 'degrees of freedom' which it might have possessed on its own. It shares only that enjoyed by the chuck itself, and as this is attached securely to the lathe mandrel (we hope) it can only move in rotation. We can, therefore, forget all about this aspect, knowing that come what may the work will rotate about the lathe axis. (Though whether this coincides with the axis of the workpiece is another matter, as we shall see). However, we pay for this advantage. In gripping the work we must inevitably cause some distortion. The forces exerted by the chuck jaws can be very large indeed if care is not taken, but even with reasonable care (and 'reasonable' means different things to different people!) the jaws must *always*

indeed, be possible to break a spoke if too great a force were applied, even from the 'light' pattern chuck shown in the photograph.

Clearly, it is necessary always to consider the cutting forces which may be applied, especially when roughing – these heavy cuts do need a secure grip. But my own practice is, where at all possible, to relax slightly the grip between roughing and finishing. There is a great deal to be said for leaving roughed-out castings or forgings for some time between the two processes, to allow locked up stresses to be relieved, and then rechucking for the finishing operation. However, if a tight grip is likely to cause distortion beyond an acceptable limit it is always prudent to reduce the cutting rate to permit a lighter grip.

How Many Jaws?

Most writers seem always to refer to the 'Independent' (or 'Universal') chuck as a 'Four-jaw' and the 'self-centering' (or 'concentric') chuck as a 'Three-jaw'. I do myself! But I have, as it happens, self-centering chucks with two, three, four and six jaws, whereas all my Independent chucks have four. So, how do we decide? Let us look at the independent or universal chuck. The requirement

Fig. 52 *Even a stiff workpiece may be affected by jaw pressure.*

here is that we must be able to move the axis of the work relative to the axis of rotation – sometimes to get the two to coincide, sometimes to provide a given degree of eccentricity. Consider Fig. 53. At (a) there are two jaws, and if these can be moved independently we can move the workpiece laterally but not up and down. However, at (b) where we have four opposing jaws in two pairs it is possible by working first on one pair and then the other to bring the center of the work O^1 to the center of

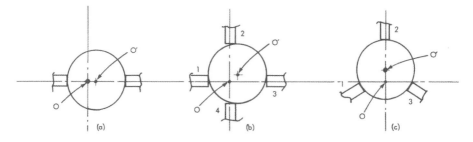

Fig. 53 *Jaw operation for a "universal" chuck. O is the center of rotation, O^1 that of the work.*

Chuckwork – General 43

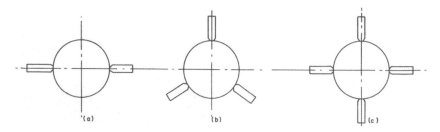

Fig. 54 *Jaw configurations for a "Self Centering" or "Concentric" chuck.*

rotation 0 without difficulty. At (c) the work is gripped in three jaws. It doesn't take long to see that to bring 0^1 down to 0 we have to slacken jaws 1 and 3 before we can tighten No. 2, and if we do that the work will fall out. It would be worse with five or more jaws. So, for the independent chuck, four jaws are essential; nothing else will do.

Now consider the requirement for 'self-centering'. The need here is for a set of jaws which are (a) equally spaced from the axis of rotation and which (b) can be moved simultaneously so that they *remain* equidistant from that axis. See Fig. 54. At (a) there are two jaws. These would hold the work central in one plane, but would need a shape at the ends (say a vee) which was inherently self centering to locate the work sideways. Such chucks *are* used in repetition work, the chuck jaws having loose pieces attached which are shaped to receive the work. At (b), with three jaws, concentricity is assured (within the limits of accuracy of the chuck) and, moreover, we are also assured of an equal force on each jaw, even if they get worn. At (c) there are four jaws. Again, concentricity is assured, but not equality of force, for the result of wear on any part may mean that one jaw may not reach. Similar considerations apply to any number of jaws, provided (a) the chuck is made so that the jaws start off concentrically, and (b) the mechanism will move all jaws the same amount. Fig. 55 shows a SIX-jaw self-centering chuck, known as a 'Bezel Chuck', as it is used chiefly for the machining of watch or clock glass bezels, though it has other uses. Clearly such a chuck must be made with great precision, and must be used with even greater care, if the six jaws are to work in harmony. These chucks are, today, very expensive – the one shown in the photo cost something over $20 in 1939.

From all this we see that the *only* combination for 'universality' is a chuck with four jaws, and the *ideal* for self-centering is three jaws, though others may have their uses. I find my self-centering four-jaw very useful indeed, especially when much work has to be done on square bar stock, but we will be looking at that point later.

Attaching the Chuck
The fixing of the chuck to the lathe mandrel is clearly of paramount importance if accuracy is to be achieved, and this is just as important for the universal as it is for the self-centering chuck. Many of the latter are supplied with the body already machined to fit the particular lathe. The user is saved the work of machining an adapter plate, and it is

claimed that greater accuracy is achieved. This may be true when the chuck is new, but the problem arises when any wear takes place. A chuck on an adapter (or 'backplate') can be adjusted, but nothing can be done with the direct fitting type. I prefer to use backplates, but this *is* a matter of opinion and preference.

It is worth while obtaining the backplate, usually (and preferably) of cast iron, with the thread and register already machined – all lathe manufacturers provide these. The user then has only to machine the face to suit the recess at the back of the chuck. The mandrel nose must be carefully – and I mean 'carefully' – cleaned and then lightly oiled. The backplate, similarly, must be scrupulously clean and if it is the first time that it has been fitted to the lathe a fairly close examination of the threads and register should be made to ensure that there are no burrs. It may fit rather tightly to the mandrel, but provided the tightness is uniform – i.e. no tight *spots* – this is an advantage rather than otherwise. If the backplate is home-made from a casting a check should be made to see that it beds uniformly over the shoulder on the mandrel. It goes without saying that equally scrupulous cleaning should be the order of the day when fitting chucks (or any accessory) to a lathe mandrel if accuracy is to be preserved.

In the case of the universal chuck the hole through the body is usually large enough to accept the screwed boss within the chuck body, with just sufficient of a boss on the other side to bed on the register collar of the mandrel (Fig. 56). This reduces the overhang on what is normally a fairly heavy chuck, and is the preferred arrangement. The holes in the body of self-centering and the smaller

Fig. 55 *A large 6-jaw Bezel chuck. The jaws are detachable, and a second set with opposite facing steps can be fitted.*

universal chucks may not allow this, and the boss must then project backwards. For this reason it is wise to specify the type of chuck for which the adapter is required.

The backplate carries a spigot which engages with a recess on the chuck and is attached with setscrews or bolts – usually the same number as there are jaws. In many books you may find the rule that the flange should bed *outside* the spigot on the universal type, and inside for the self-centering. This is not necessarily true. The requirement is that the flange should bed flat down on *that part of the chuck through which the bolts pass,* so that if on, say, a four-jaw chuck the P.C.D. of the bolts lies within the spigot recess, then the flanges should bed there, with a clearance of say 0.005 in. elsewhere. This is to ensure that no distortion is caused when tightening the fixing bolts. Note the recesses and clearances shown on

Chuckwork – General 45

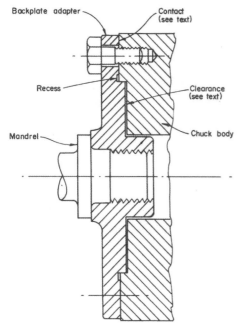

Fig. 56. *Backplate adapter with register thread within the chuck body.*

Fig. 56. It is most important that the chuck body can sit down on the face of the backplate.

There is always debate about the fit on the spigot itself. There can be no argument in the case of the universal chuck; the spigot should fit and fit well, so that the outside diameter of the heavy chuck runs true. For any self-centering chuck, however, I believe that the balance of the argument is in favor of a little clearance on the spigot – just a few thousandths of an inch – so that the chuck can be set with work in the jaws to give the least amount of runout. All chucks are made to a tolerance, typically 0.003 in. total indicator reading, and a 'dead true' chuck can be no more than luck!

Once fitted, the jaws must be removed and the *face* of the chuck checked for accuracy. This is very important, whatever the type of chuck, for we rely on the face (and sometimes on the faces of the steps of the jaws) for setting up work in service. If there is any error then the face of the backplate must be scraped to correct it – always assuming that the machining has been correct in the first place. The check must be made by rotating the chuck under the dial indicator, not by traversing it across the face, as the machine should be arranged to turn slightly concave when facing, as we noted when dealing with faceplates.

46 WORKHOLDING IN THE LATHE FOR HOME MACHINISTS

CHAPTER 4

The Universal or Independent Chuck

This is a development from the use of dogs on the faceplate and is illustrated in books on turning going back for centuries – see Fig. 57. There are two alternative types of construction on the modern version. Some have threaded adjusting screws working in threads in the body which move with the jaws, the screw being removed entirely when the jaw is to be reversed. This construction is confined to small, very light pattern chucks, and the screws are often of vee form. More usually the screw is captive in the body of the chuck and the thread, of square form, engages with part threads on the back of the jaw. Fig. 58 shows the two types, one a 4 in. and the other 6 in., both of which are termed the 'light' pattern. The captive screw type is much stronger and is preferred for general work, but the other type is both lighter and cheaper and takes up less room – it is shallower. The captive screw type can be had in

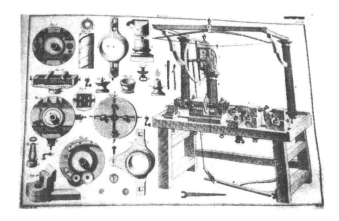

Fig. 57 *Illustration of a lathe of about 1780, showing a four-jaw independent chuck just to the left of the bed.*

The Universal or Independent Chuck   47

Fig. 58 *Left: A 6-inch chuck with captive screws.*
Right: A 4-inch chuck, the screws traveling with the jaws.

sizes from about 2 in. dia. upwards (Fig. 59), but the other is seldom made above 4 in. dia., Fig. 60 shows another type.

The normal or preferred size as standard fitting for a center lathe (other considerations apply to capstans) is that which will permit the chuck to hold work equal in diameter to the chuck body without the jaws fouling the lathe bed. (Few chucks will hold work in the normal gap). For a 3½ in. lathe this implies a body 6 in. diameter. The 4 in. size is half the weight and about half the price of a 6 in., so that, provided you are *sure* that no large or relatively heavy work is to be done, the smaller size will be adequate. Chuck bodies may be of steel or H.T. cast iron. There is little point in a steel body for amateur work, and the 'heavy duty' chucks are designed for work heavier than the lathe will take, so far as the average amateur machine is concerned!

Gripping Force

The Universal chuck – or whatever name you care to give to it – acquires merit from its ability to work at the two

Fig. 59 *A small – 2-inch – independent chuck with captive screws.*

Fig. 60 *An independent chuck with non-reversible jaws; there are steps facing both ways. The machine is a 65mm "LORCH".*

extremes. On the one hand it can provide a secure hold of heavy irregularly-shaped workpieces, while on the other it is the *only* workholder in which previously turned pieces can be reset axially true with precision. It is *not* a device 'for rough work only' and it should be treated with the respect it deserves. In far too many cases an examination of a second hand lathe outfit reveals damaged chuck screw sockets or twisted square ends on the key – all evidence of misuse. There should never be any occasion to use enough force to cause either. The relative sizes of chuck key and the diameter and pitch of the screws are such that, were there no friction in the guides, the jaws of a light 6 in. chuck could exert a force on the workpiece of about 8 tons when applied with reasonable hand pressure. By setting a piece of mild steel of known cross-section between one pair of jaws I was able to measure the change in length when the grip was increased from 'just holding' to what I would regard as 'reasonable' – the key being turned with one hand only. The deflection corresponded to an axial load in the test piece of 3430 lbf – just over 1½ tons; enough for most purposes! There is no need to extend the key with bits of pipe, still less to do what was suggested a few years ago, adapt a belly-brace to fit the screw sockets!

Setting the work

The variety of shapes which are held in the universal chuck make it difficult to suggest any rules, but there are some which may help, and I hope that the few examples which I shall illustrate may assist further. The first point to observe is that when setting up castings or forgings the work should be adjusted so that the parts which will remain *unmachined* run true. On a flywheel this might be the inner circumference of the rim, or the boss (or compromise between the two). On an engine cylinder, the outside of the bore – the boring tool will look after the inside. At the same time, it is always prudent to lay a few dimensions over the rough casting to ensure that the machining allowances are fairly shared out. Taking an engine cylinder as example again, the amount to come off the flanges at each end should be balanced so that they end up more or less the same thickness. Fig. 61 shows the rough casting for a brass cupchuck for my Holtzapffel lathe set up, and it can be seen that the boss and the O.D. are not co-axial (Look at the chalkmarks). The chuck was adjusted to ensure that there would be both sufficient metal to form the boss, and a wall thickness adequate for the duty.

It saves a lot of time if the work can be 'rough set' first – I often do this on the bench before mounting chuck and work together on the lathe mandrel. To this end most universal chucks are machined with circular setting lines on

Fig. 61 *Centering a casting, using chalk marks.*

The Universal or Independent Chuck 49

the body. If these are not there, then they can be machined in with a pointed tool after the chuck is first set up. In many cases – the casting in Fig. 61, for example – it is sufficient to set up the work using chalk held against the rotating workpiece; the jaw opposite the mark should be slackened and then its opposite mate tightened. It is quicker to work on one pair of jaws at a time rather than to hop from one pair to the other. On a 6 in. chuck a 45 deg. turn of the key will move the work about 0.015 in. – equivalent to a runout of 1/32 inch.

If great accuracy is required (and some shell-molded castings are so true that very little machining is needed) use a round-end rod (or even a tool) in the toolpost and read the setting of the cross-slide index when it touches the work on the opposite side. The point should be applied in line with the chuck jaws, of course. The difference between the two readings is *twice* the amount that the jaws must be moved. With this procedure (Fig. 62) a very rapid setting can be achieved, though I usually use chalk in the first instance. I need not say that a dial indicator should NOT be used on a rough casting, but its use is almost imperative when resetting previously turned work. The test pin method (or even the use of the tool point in the same way) will give results as good as resetting in a standard self-centering chuck – or better – but for exactitude you need a very sensitive 'feel' and a very easy-running cross-slide. It is important to check *both* axial and radial truth. In the case of a wheel, the D.T.I. must be applied both to the circumference *and* the face of the rim, and for a cylinder, on the diameter and length of the bore. Work held within the jaws can be very difficult, and on occasion I have found it necessary to use shim-steel at one end or other of one or more jaws; a tedious business, but the only way if real accuracy is required. Bear in mind my previous remarks about jaw pressure – it is always tempting to move that last half-mil by tightening just one jaw, but all that has been done is to squeeze in the workpiece!

You may notice in some of my photos that two jaws adjacent to each other are marked with yellow paint. This is to aid repetition work in the 4-jaw, for example, when a number of columns

Fig. 62 *Centering work using a contact pin in conjunction with the cross-slide index.*

50 WORKHOLDING IN THE LATHE FOR HOME MACHINISTS

are to be machined from square stock. If these two jaws alone are released when changing workpieces the next will be held pretty close to the previous setting, though again, for accurate work it is prudent to check. Here a word about holding square work may be opposite. Look at Fig. 63. It is possible to get a good grip, as you may believe, with the work disposed as shown. There are two hazards. First, the work may shift under the successive blows from the tool during what will be an interrupted cut. Second, if another piece is then set up it will not run true. The trick is to apply very little jaw pressure in the first instance and to 'wobble the work about' until you feel that the square is held in the center of its flats. (The same condition can apply to hexagonal stock held in a chuck with three jaws.)

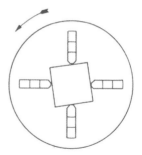

Fig. 63 *Cutting tool forces on the workpiece corners may cause the work to rotate within the jaws which may then lose their grip.*

Irregular shaped work

It is in the nature of model engineering that many of the castings we handle are an awkward shape, for we use the center lathe to machine jobs which, in Industry, would be dealt with either in special machines or in expensive fixtures. In many cases these castings are provided with 'chucking pieces' – projections with which to hold the work but which are finally cut away. It is unfortunate that the casting process is such that the bosses are frequently not true to the workpiece proper, and often inadequate in size as well. Fig 64 is a case in point, the chucking piece lying at an angle to the main body. In most cases I set up the work so that the first operation is the machining of the chucking-piece itself; I then have a reasonable chance of setting the work later. However, in this case the casting can be held without using the chucking

Fig. 64 *A tender-pump casting on which the chucking piece is askew.*

Fig. 65 *The casting in Fig. 64 held without using the chucking piece.*

Fig. 66 *A piece of scrap has been brazed to the heel of the bend to assist in providing a better grip.*

Fig. 67 *Chucking work with one jaw reversed.*

iron flanged bend and there was no chance of getting a casting in reasonable time. So, a commercial bend was machined so that flanges could be brazed on and then the flanges themselves machined. Holding such a bend in a chuck is difficult, as the jaw on the back of the curve tended to slip. A piece of scrap steel was brazed on and this solved the difficulty.

The jaws of universal chucks can be reversed, and there is no reason at all why all should point the same way; one or more may be reversed to hold a difficult workpiece. Fig. 67 shows the pump body of Fig. 64 set up as it would be for machining the valve cavity. One jaw is reversed. Had the casting been held right back against the face of the chuck this jaw would have fouled the lathe bed, so the flange rests on one of the steps. Obviously care must be taken that all is square. Incidentally, this set up is badly out of balance for the speed at which the machine *ought* to be run, and at least partial balance should have been applied. (The photo was, of course, 'set up' for the purpose of this

piece at all (Fig. 65) provided a check for squareness of the base flange is made both ways. A square held on the chuck jaw will serve, sighting the blade and the flange 'by eye'.

Chucking pieces can be added to castings (or even bar stock) to aid holding, if need be. I have used soft solder, Araldite, and brazing – or even drilled and tapped a hole for a screw on small jobs. Fig. 66 is an example. A model required a 'scale' cast

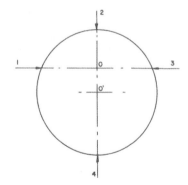

Fig. 68 *Circular work held eccentrically in a four jaw chuck. Any movement of the work, center 0', upwards requires all three jaws 1, 2, 3, to be slackened. Movement downwards causes 2 and 3 to lose grip.*

52 WORKHOLDING IN THE LATHE FOR HOME MACHINISTS

book – I haven't made a 5 in. gauge locomotive for over 30 years, but can't bring myself to melt down this casting!) To attach a balance weight I have one or two flat strips of steel with tapped holes in them. These strips fit in the slide grooves in the chuck body, and weights can be attached with Allen screws.

Fig. 68 illustrates a problem which arises when circular work is held off center. This is a 'variation' of the case shown in Fig 53(c). Any adjustment in the vertical direction requires attention to jaws 1 and 3, as well as the other two. If the offset is considerable the set up will be unstable; pressure on jaws 1 and 3 is magnified by the geometry and could be enough to reduce that exerted by jaw 2 to zero. There is also risk of marking the work and packing is desirable under jaws 1 and 3. There is no way out of this problem other than marking a fixture (though I do show in Fig. 75 an unusual expedient, later!) and as long as the situation is recognized it need not be serious.

Overhang

I find that many model engineers are apprehensive when holding work with any degree of overhang from the chuck. Fig. 69 is a case in point. Here the column of a vertical engine (the *Williamson*) is being machined and bored to fit the base spigot. It looks formidable, though the length/diameter ratio is only about 2½/1. More important, there is a robust flange at the chuck end on which a good grip can be obtained. Had this not been so, a dummy center – wooden or lead – would have been fitted in the hole for tailstock support while the outer diameter was turned, after which the end could be supported in the fixed steady rest for boring. It is just not possible to give any 'rule' in cases like

these; judgement – and, perhaps, courage! – must be applied. If the initial cut must be heavy, or the cut irregular, a dummy center is usually prudent, but on the other hand too light a cut may result in chatter. Fig. 70 shows the means adopted for the other end of the same casting. A steel blank is held in the chuck and machined with a spigot to fit the column, and with a hole through the center. The casting is drawn back on this with a drawbar through the mandrel, with a cross-bar through the

Fig. 69 *This tall casting has been successfully machined despite the overhang.*

Fig. 70 *The casting of Fig. 69 secured to a spigot-block using a crosspiece and drawbar.*

The Universal or Independent Chuck 53

Fig. 71 *A tall cylinder gripped by the barrel using packing under the jaws. Care must be taken to avoid distorton due to jaw pressure.*

apertures of the column. This is a very useful arrangement, and one which I use when re-machining pistons, the eye end of the drawbar engaging with a dummy gudgeon pin.

Fig. 71 shows a long beam engine cylinder set up for facing and boring. To reduce the overhang the jaws grip the cylinder body, not the top flange, with packing pieces interposed. This illustrates again the point already mentioned – it is imperative that both ends of the casting be checked for truth otherwise the bore will be 'slantendicular'. This type of machining would perhaps be best done with a boring bar between centers, the casting on the cross-slide, but my boring bar was just too large to enter. Once the outer flange had been machined the steady rest was again used for both boring and facing, the problem being that chatter developed at the final boring cuts.

Unorthodox arrangements

Fig. 72 shows a set up illustrated in almost all books on turning, where a slab of material is to be reduced in width. Current practice would be to use the vertical slide and an endmill, but there are occasions where this is not possible. The arrangement is perfectly legitimate and despite the interrupted cut the grip will be adequate. However, care must be taken not to overtighten the jaws. And on no account should the work be held at the extremities of the jaws – it should bed down on the chuck face. Fig. 73 shows the reason. The jaws feel considerable side-pressure and, if this is applied towards the top of the step, there will be undue strain on the lip of the jaw guide in the cast body. Fig. 74 is a set up which I have found very handy when a number of eccentrically turned or bored workpieces are needed. A small self-centering chuck – three or four jaw, depending on whether the stock is round or square – is held in the universal chuck and set eccentric as needed. Thereafter, all changes of workpiece are made on the self-centering chuck. There is, of course, considerable out of balance, so that speeds must be kept within reason, but the time lost in using low cutting

Fig. 72 *A slab held between the angles of the jaws. This can strain the guides.*

54 WORKHOLDING IN THE LATHE FOR HOME MACHINISTS

speeds is more than made up by the saving in setting up time. As a matter of interest, combined self-centering and 'universal' chucks *are* available – at a price! – commercially, but these have the self-centering facility behind the universal jaws. I haven't priced one for a long time, but they were roughly three times the price of a 3-jaw self-centering chuck of the same diameter. I *have* on occasion used a machine vice held in the chuck, and Fig. 75 shows an application of vee-blocks in the chuck which I have seen used in industry on a repair job, but never used myself. It does offer a solution to the problem of Fig. 68, perhaps!

Fig. 74 *A self-centering chuck held offset in the independent chuck.*

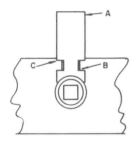

Fig. 73 *End view of a chuck jaw. A force at A imposes strains at faces B and C and across the section between.*

more complaints about 'inaccurate' self-centering chucks. I shall be dealing with this in the next chapter, but the short point is that the 'three-jaw' is not *intended* to be a *precise* accessory; it is meant for *convenience* when holding circular or hexagonal barstock. The independent chuck is much underused

Universal chuck – Conclusions

The Universal or Independent chuck should be the 'first buy' so far as lathe accessories are concerned (after the cutting tools, of course!). It can do *all* that the self-centering chuck can do except center automatically. It is true that centering will take time, but it will be more accurate and, what is more, the very act of centering will indicate the error, if any. It can hold a very wide variety of shapes and, where necessary, get a really good grip when such force is necessary. I hear many and read even

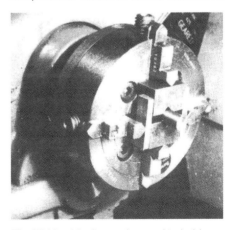

Fig. 75 *Vee-blocks can be used to hold offset work in the 4-jaw chuck.*

The Universal or Independent Chuck 55

by the amateur engineer.

In choosing a chuck, regard should be taken of the average class of work likely to be undertaken. For a 3½ in. lathe the 6 in. 'light' pattern with iron body is the general choice. There is no point in going for a 'heavy duty' chuck on a lathe which will not take sufficiently heavy cuts to load it fully. However, both the 3 in. and the 4 in. dia. chucks have their uses. The small watchmaker's independent chucks, with 'steps facing both ways' (the jaws do not reverse) have little application outside their specialist field, but I DO regret the fact that no manufacturers now supply chucks with four steps on the jaws; all seem to have but three. My 'grandfather' four-jaw, supplied with my first Myford (No. K3020, if anyone cares to date it!) had four steps, and I have had many occasions to congratulate myself on keeping it when the lathe was sold.

CHAPTER 5

The Self-centering Chuck

The name is a misnomer, for the chuck does not center itself, but rather holds the work concentric to the lathe axis – within the limits of accuracy of the device. This is why early works on the lathe refer to 'Concentric' chucks; however, usage must have its way, and in what follows the current name will be used. Abbreviated to S/c, perhaps, but for reasons already given it is unwise to use the term 'Three-jaw'; it may have more and can have less!

The device is very old, and chucks resembling those of a carpenter's brace are described in very early books. These were later developed into sophisticated forms and became known as 'Die-chucks' – 'Die' being the term used to describe the moving gripping jaws, and with no connection with the modern threading die. These all held relatively small workpieces, and it was not until the beginning of the 19th century, when more or less repetition work appeared on the scene, that a truly concentric chuck appeared. This is seen in Fig. 76. The view on the left shows the front of the chuck, with three dogs sliding in radial grooves, these dogs being so arranged that they can grip either on the outside or the inside of a workpiece. The worm seen in the righthand view rotates a plate cut with three grooves in the shape of part circles, these grooves engaging with pins on the back of the dogs. As this plate is rotated by the worm the dogs move inwards or outwards in unison. Another form, dating from 1818, is seen in Fig. 77. The idea is similar, but the 'jaws' are also restrained by radial arms, thus doing away with the necessity for the vee-grooves of the previous example.

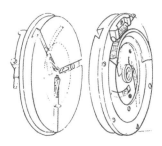

Fig. 76 *A very early self-centering chuck. The right-hand view has the backplate removed.*

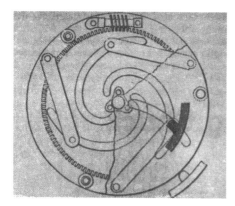

Fig. 77 *Another early chuck. The workholding dog (one of three) is shown shaded, with a detail at the bottom right hand side.*

(The milling machine had not been invented at this time.)

The self-centering two-jaw chuck has already been mentioned. Fig. 78 shows my own, dated about 1825, in which the jaws are moved by action of left- and right-hand threads on a central spindle. The jaws are removable and different shapes and curvatures can be fitted to suit different work. In a later type of the same style the jaws were in the form of square blocks with a different size of vee on each face, which could be brought into play by rotating the block. This had the advantage of giving a fairly accurate centering of square workpieces.

The Scroll chuck – the type we know today – was invented by a Scot, James Dundas, in 1842, in the form shown in Fig. 79. The rear plate, carried on the mandrel nose, is machined with a continuous spiral groove, and the backs of the jaws are made with teeth which engage with this spiral. The front part has three grooves in which the jaws fit and is arranged so that it can be rotated relative to the backplate. This

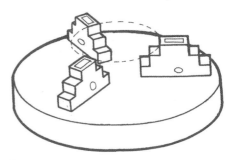

Fig. 79 *One of the earliest scroll chucks. The grooves are hidden beneath the jaws, which "face both ways".*

rotation causes the spiral to move the jaws in or out. The jaws are made with steps to grip both inside and outside the workpiece as needed, the jaws not being reversible.

This principle is the basis of all manually operated concentric chucks today, the main difference being that the scroll is rotated, rather than the chuck body, when effecting movement of the jaws. It is as well, therefore, to examine the action of this mechanism, so that the limitations (both as regards accuracy and strength of grip) can be understood. Readers who have such a chuck

Fig. 78 *A Holtapffel 2-jaw self-centering chuck of about 1830. The jaws can be exchanged for others of different shape.*

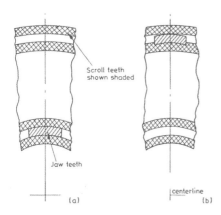
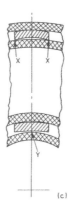
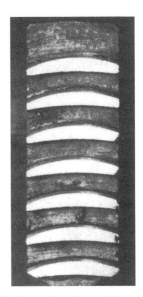

Fig. 80 *Engagement of jaw teeth with the scroll. A tooth which fits properly at (a) will suffer interference when at (b) and the edges of the hard jaw teeth will dig in. This has been overcome at (c) by providing more clearance, but results in two-point contact at "x" changing to single contact at "y". The jaw would "fit" at one point only.*

Fig. 81 *Jaw teeth of a modern chuck. The curvature is such that single-point contact is maintained throughout.*

handy may care to take out the jaws and examine them, but Fig. 80 will show the main points. It is immediately apparent that as the scroll is a 'spiral' – a curve of continuously changing radius – it is impossible to machine a series of teeth on the back of the jaws which will properly fit the scroll if the jaw is to move across the radius. On early chucks by Cushman and others the shape of the jaw teeth was such that they 'fitted' reasonably well over a jaw travel corresponding to the distance between the work-holding steps, and the workpiece should have been moved to the next step if greater jaw movement were required. Even so, it is evident from Fig. 80 that the teeth would jam unless considerable clearance or backlash was provided and this was a feature of the early scroll chucks.

Fig. 81 shows the shape of the teeth on a modern chuck. It will be seen that the outer face is machined to a radius slightly smaller than the smallest radius of the scroll, and the inner to one slightly larger than the largest. The thickness of the tooth at its center is a slide fit to the groove in the scroll, so that backlash is almost absent – when new. Examination of a chuck jaw will show that contact with the scroll always occurs over a small area at the center of each tooth. (After some time for the teeth to bed down.) The backlash increases slightly (which is not important) and over the most commonly used range of workpiece size contact is distributed over this bedded area. At extremes of jaw travel – right in or right out – there will still be no more than line contact between scroll and tooth.

The Self-centering Chuck 59

Fig. 82 *A geared scroll self-centering chuck.*

Types of Chuck

Figs. 82 to 85 show the three common forms of the scroll chuck. Fig. 82 is the 'Geared Scroll' type, shown dismantled in Fig. 83. (The latter is my fairly old 'Burnerd' ready for its annual clean-up.) The cast-iron body has a center core on which the scroll can rotate with the minimum of bearing clearance. This core also has three holes in which the pegs on the inner end of the three (in this case) hard steel bevel pinions are located. These small pinions engage with a larger bevel on the back of the tough steel scroll. Both scroll and pinions are retained within the body by the cast-iron retaining plate seen on the right of the photo. I have set a pinion in place against each of the three components to make matters a bit clearer. Operation of any of the pinions will cause the scroll to rotate and so move the jaws. This type of chuck usually has two sets of jaws, for internal and external gripping.

Fig. 84 shows the 'Hand-grip Scroll Chuck', much used on watchmaker's lathes. In this case the scroll is rotated by the knurled ring. The front part is separate from the back, with the scroll, which runs on a center stem as before, sandwiched between. Naturally, the grip obtained is much smaller, but is more than adequate for the class of work involved. With these chucks the jaws are attached to sliding members by small screws, and the jaws can be detached and reversed as needed. (Or top parts of a different shape can be fitted.) The operation is much quicker and, though most small lathes of this type are designed for use with collets, the chuck has the advantage that it can hold rings or discs and is cheaper

Fig. 83 *Parts of a geared scroll chuck. Top left, scroll, with pinion engaged with the bevel on the back. Center, top; chuck body. The scroll rotates on the center column. The body is held to the mandrel backplate by three setscrews in the holes on its periphery. Top right, pinion retainer, which also serves to hold the scroll against the front inner face of the body. Below, the two alternative sets of jaws.*

(though not necessarily less accurate) than the set of ten step-chucks which provide the alternative.

Fig. 85 is a derivation of the Handgrip chuck, known as the 'Lever Scroll Chuck'. The difference is that the operating ring can be turned by applying a lever in one of several holes on the periphery. This gives a stronger hold, and such chucks can be had in much larger sizes – up to about 4 in. diameter. Another difference is that they are usually provided with two sets of jaws in the same fashion as is the geared scroll chuck. Though providing a stronger grip than the handgrip type they cannot compare with the geared scroll, and their main application is where rapid changes of workpiece are needed in very light turning or in grinding operations.

Strength of Concentric Chucks

The torque magnification provided by the bevel drive on a geared scroll chuck is about 3.7:1 (most have the gear ratio arranged to give a 'hunting tooth' on the scroll, to equalize wear) and the effective wedge/angle of the scroll on a 4 in. chuck varies from about $\frac{1}{5}$ to $\frac{1}{10}$. Despite this variation, the force on the jaw teeth is sensibly constant over the full travel – the change in wedge effect is compensated for by the change in radius of action of the applied torque. Friction takes its toll, and will absorb some of the torque applied to the chuck key, but with 'reasonable' force applied with two hands the thrust on *each* jaw could be of the order of one ton. The 'thread' of the scroll of the normal 4 in. chuck is about 0.085 in. wide and no more than three threads are engaged with any jaw. Even with 'normal' tightening, the stress in the scroll is high and the contact pressure between scroll and jaw teeth very high indeed.

Fig. 84 *A 2-inch hand-grip scroll chuck, for a watchmaker's lathe. The jaws are held to the sliding members by small screws.*

The strength of the normal pattern self-centering chuck used by the model engineer is adequate for the class of work for which it was designed, but it does have its limitations and these should be kept in mind. It may be

Fig. 85 *A lever-scroll chuck. Similar to that in Fig. 84 but larger and provided with holes for a tommy-bar on the scroll.*

taken as a universal truth that if work slips in the jaws, then the cutting forces are too high. The correct remedy is to reduce these forces, not to apply a piece of pipe to the chuck key – nor to use more 'heft'. Apart from risk of damage to the chuck the workpiece may well be distorted if too much force is applied. For the majority of turning jobs a 'one-hand' application of the key should suffice.

This point about 'reasonable force' cannot be too strongly emphasized. The weakest part of the chuck is the scroll; there can be no force applied without some deflection, and too much may result in uneven deflection of the scroll so that concentricity is lost. If so much force is applied as to cause a permanent set in the scroll then accuracy is lost for ever. There is no way of rectifying it.

Accuracy

Just as most model engineers expect their lathe to do work far in excess of that for which it was designed, so they seem to expect unreasonable degrees of accuracy from their chucks! The main purpose of the self-centering chuck is to hold round or hexagonal stock *reasonably* true with the minimum of effort. It is a 'tool of convenience'. The 'normal' workpiece envisaged was one which would be finished and parted off at one setting but which was too short to hold between centers. Some pieces might have unmachined parts – hexagon bolts, for example – but in this case a slight eccentricity of the unmachined part would not matter. In normal manufacturing neither the Designer nor the Production Engineer would expect to *reverse* the work in the chuck – apart, perhaps, for a simple end-facing operation; and even this would normally

be carried out on a 'second operation' machine.

The model engineer has no such second machine. Further, the 'scale effect' means that his components are so small that there is often no chance of finishing all at one setting. So, he looks for a degree of precision from his workholder that is not there. *All chucks are made to tolerances.* Jaws are made in one section of the works, scrolls in another, and bodies elsewhere again. It is true that 'selective assembly' is practiced, to eliminate gross errors, but the guaranteed centricity of a *standard* 4 in. chuck is no better than about 3 thousandths of an inch T.I.R. (Total Indicator Reading.) The *repeatability* will be better than this – that is, the change in T.I.R. on stock of the same diameter is usually better than 0.0015 inch. But if the workpiece is turned about, and held at a different chuck jaw setting, then you may well be finding your D.T.I. indicating a total runout of more than 3 mil, even on a new chuck perfectly acceptable to British Standard No. 1983. (Most will, by the laws of chance, be better than this, but none worse, when new.) To make standard chucks to closer tolerances would add so much to the cost as to make them prohibitive.

Precision chucks *are* available. These have nitrogen hardened and ground scrolls, the jaws are ground on the teeth, jaws and on the slideways; the body also is ground on the slideways. The performance is not only better – 0.0015 in. T.I.R. – but will also remain so for much longer. Further, there seems to be less variation in the eccentricity over the range of grip. They are, of course, more expensive than the 'Standard' but not that much more so. It should be noted that there are some continental chucks of reputable make

62 WORKHOLDING IN THE LATHE FOR HOME MACHINISTS

available where the actual construction of the standard and the precision chucks is identical. But each chuck is given an individual test (and a certificate provided) and those which pass out with a T.I.R. better than 0.001 in. are classed as 'precision'.

The 'Griptru' Chuck

The practice of mounting a concentric chuck in the jaws of a four-jaw independent chuck in order to achieve absolute repeatability has already been mentioned. Later, a 'Combination Chuck' was introduced which was, in effect, the same thing, but all contrived in the one unit. This was expensive and really only justified where repetition *eccentric* work was in hand. It was far too complex and costly a device to be acceptable to correct a TIR of the order of 0.002 in. To meet this need the Griptru chuck was introduced, and is shown in Fig. 86. (The photograph, Fig. 87, is of a six-jaw chuck, but shows the

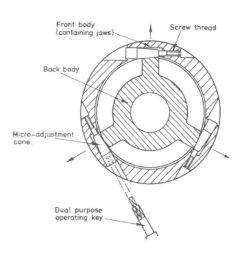

Fig. 86 *Diagram illustrating the operation of a Griptru chuck. The back body is attached to the lathe mandrel nose. The front body can move very slightly in the radial direction relative to the back body. Movement is controlled by the cones. The arrows show the direction of movement of the work when the adjacent cone is screwed inwards.*

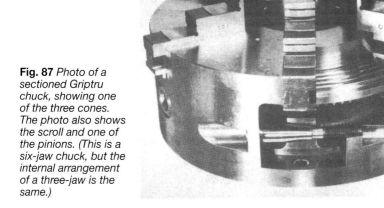

Fig. 87 *Photo of a sectioned Griptru chuck, showing one of the three cones. The photo also shows the scroll and one of the pinions. (This is a six-jaw chuck, but the internal arrangement of a three-jaw is the same.)*

The Self-centering Chuck 63

mechanism just the same.) The body, carrying the jaws, is free to move on the backplate by a very small amount radially, but is restrained in the axial direction. The photograph shows a conical wedge adjacent to the jaw in the foreground. There are three of these, one between each pair of operating pinions. (See Fig. 87.) Each wedge can be advanced or retracted under the influence of the thread on the end, when operated by a key. If, after chucking, the work is found to run out, two of the cones are retracted and the third advanced to correct the runout. Once this has been done the work can confidently be expected to show a repeatability of 0.0005 in. and individual settings to 0.0002 in. are possible. It should be noted, however, that the scroll is not hardened or ground, and the cone settings have usually to be altered if the diameter of the grip is changed; correction at one jaw setting is *not* necessarily maintained over the full range of jaw travel.

It is important to remember first, that if one cone is adjusted to move the body inwards, then the other two must first be retracted to allow the body to move. It is, in fact, preferable to start the adjustment with all three cones in the 'slack' position. In other words, the practice should be the same as would be used with an independent chuck. Secondly, the front body is, of course, held to the backbody or core by screws as on a normal chuck. These are, as a rule, adjusted to be tight enough to hold securely, but not so tight as to prevent the cones from performing their office. The cones will hold the body radially when all are bearing. In time these screws will 'work tight' and the adjustment may be difficult. When this happens the chuck should be dismantled and cleaned, and the screws then readjusted to give firm, but not total restraint.

Care must be taken when using the Griptru at high speeds – 2000 r.p.m. or over. The body is necessarily out of balance, and it may be found that chatter can develop due to the consequent vibration.

The Nominated Key Socket

All chuck makers guarantee their accuracy only when the 'nominated socket' is used for the key. A simple test will serve to show that the degree of concentricity achieved does vary according to which pinion is used to tighten the jaws. The reason is simple. The scroll rotates on the center core of the backplate and must have a slight clearance there. Further, there must also be a slight clearance between scroll and body in the axial direction. Thus the scroll *can* move relative to the axis of rotation of the chuck. The pinions themselves are a fairly free fit in the body and of a relatively coarse pitch. In service, therefore, each pinion is likely to displace the scroll radially by a different amount. The 'Nominated' pinion is that which has the least effect – as measured by a dial indicator on the workpiece.

Interestingly enough, the precision chucks on my Lorch lathe have but one pinion. There is, therefore, no possibility of variation of error between pinions. And once one knows the degree of error this can be corrected when mounting the chuck (or, as in this case, at the inspection stage when the chuck is made).

It must be remarked that the 'Nomination' will not remain the same through the life of the chuck, and may not apply to the alternate set of jaws either. My own practice is to mark the preferred socket with paint rather than with a number stamp. It is then an easy matter to change the mark should this prove necessary. I always check the 'preference' at each annual check-over on the lathe, and occasionally in between as well.

Sources of Error, and Correction
The most common source of error is, as has already been suggested, overstraining of the scroll. Once this occurs nothing can be done to effect a permanent cure. Even a fractional change of jaw position will result in a considerable change in concentricity. New jaws will not help, either. If the chuck is backplate fitted, then the best expedient is to machine the spigot to provide a clearance to the recess on the chuck. The work can then be brought concentric, after tightening the jaws, by careful blows of a rawhide mallet on the chuck body. A crude form of Griptru! This is a method not to be disdained and all my backplates are so arranged. This enables me to set up my chucks, so that the TIR at 1 in. work diameter when using the nominated socket is better than 0.0005 in.

However, if the chuck is made to screw direct onto the mandrel nose this cannot be done. The only solution then is to apply shims under one or more jaws of the chuck. Again, a perfectly legitimate procedure, given that the chuck has an error. Indeed, it is a means I use when deliberately needing an eccentric workpiece, as I shall describe later, so why not use it to turn true as well?

An error due to age may be due to scroll wear (as opposed to the distortion mentioned above) or to wear on the jaw teeth. To determine which is the most likely, make a series of measurements with a DTI at three different settings of the jaws, say about half an inch apart, and using the same socket for each. Now change to the much less used outside jaws and do the same. The jaws should cover roughly the same part of the scroll in each case. If the TIR at each setting is *markedly* better with the less-used jaws, then it may be assumed that jaw wear is the culprit. If, however, the difference is small then the scroll is worn. If the readings show no consistency at all – some better, some worse, then it must be assumed that both scroll and jaws are at fault.

Replacement jaws can be obtained for most chucks, but it is hardly worth while until the gripping faces themselves have become worn beyond reason. (A good indication is that when parting-off close to the chuck jaws the work shows signs of 'workpiece rattle'. This shows that the stock is being gripped only at the back of the jaw.) However, both the mechanics of the chuck and experience suggest that though the scroll may wear it usually does so fairly evenly over the length provided it has never been overstrained, and I must confess that when I have been able to check I have usually found jaw wear to be the culprit. The alternative to replacing the jaw is, as above, to use shims under one or more jaws, or to adjust the chuck on its backplate each time it is used.

Wear in the jaw slides is unlikely to cause radial error until the slides are so bad that the chuck is, in fact, worn out, but a troublesome and erratic error can arise from the presence of a *burr* on the slide in the body. The very slightest movement of the jaw in the region of this burr will give a startling change in concentricity – or lack of it. Similar effects will result from trapped swarf or

The Self-centering Chuck   65

even hard dirt. The remedy is to stone off the offending burr in the first instance, and to keep the chuck clean in the second!

Chuck Jaws

Two sets of jaws are normally provided, one with the ground gripping faces pointing outwards, but with a gripping face at the smallest diameter as well. These are often regarded as the 'normal' jaws; both barstock and rings or hollow workpieces can be held. The other set has all gripping faces pointing inwards, for use on larger diameter material – and, of course, for rings gripped on the outside diameter. In both types, however, the outer extremity of the jaw is NOT intended for use. It is not ground, and although it may *hold* large, hollow work it will not do so accurately. In judging which jaws to use, the rule should be that at no time should the scroll be disengaged from any of the jaw teeth. With the normal 4 in. chuck this limits the jaw travel to an extension outside the body by about ¼ in. or a little more. A *light* grip may be applied with the jaws projecting by perhaps ½ in., (Fig. 88) but the scroll

Fig. 88 *How to ruin a chuck! Only two teeth of the scroll are engaged and the force needed to hold a workpiece this size will distort it. A 4-jaw "universal" chuck should be used.*

engagement is then limited and the risk of distortion is increased.

Soft jaws are much used for repetition work in industry, the faces being machined to suit the work in hand. These are usually two-part jaws, a permanent hard piece with flat top sliding in the body to which the soft working top can be attached with bolts. They do have their uses for model engineers, and a suggestion is shown in Fig. 89. The soft (steel) adapter must be held firmly by the setscrews, must fit well on the sides of the hard jaws, and have a recess as shown in which a disc can be gripped to hold the soft jaws in firm contact with the hard ones when boring them. I have used such once or twice over the years, but would not find them worth while making up unless several dozen identical workpieces had to be machined. If it is likely that such repetition work will be frequent, then it is best to buy the chuck with soft jaws in the first instance. The replacement jaws are very cheap indeed (relative to the cost of the normal ones).

Rectifying Worn Jaws

In time the inner face of the barstock jaws ('normal' jaws) will wear, especially if a great deal of work has been gripped at the extremity instead of full length. Most articles describing the regrinding of these faces require a ring to be set at the back of the jaws (as recommended above in relation to the soft jaw) to ensure that the jaw is hard up against the scroll during grinding. This is not necessary. The outer gripping faces are, when new, concentric to the inner faces within the tolerance of the chuck, and these faces are not subject to any appreciable wear. It is, therefore, necessary only to chuck a substantial truly machined ring on the inner of the outward facing of the jaws – I suggest of such a diameter that the outer ends of the jaws are flush with the body – and tighten the jaws against this before grinding. The operation does demand a toolpost grinder of reasonable quality and some care in use. It is helpful to set the topslide over at an angle of about 5 deg. to the lathe axis and use this to set on the 'cut'. One mil travel of the topslide will then give one tenth mil depth of cut on the grinding wheel. It is to be observed that it is very unlikely that the accuracy can be improved above that which the chuck possessed when new, but the pestilential nuisance of jaws which will grip even long bar stock only at the back *can* be abated!

Eccentric Work in the Concentric Chuck
To the 'Ornamental' turner an eccentric chuck is a normal piece of equipment, and there are many occasions when such a device would be useful to the model engineer. I have already mentioned one method – to set the self-centering chuck in the jaws of the independent chuck and adjust the latter to give the required offset. The only disadvantage is that the out-of-balance is considerable and it is difficult to attain normal cutting speeds (needed for reasonable finish) even on small offsets. For machining the boss and bore of a steam engine eccentric the necessary offset can be obtained by setting packing under one (or, if more convenient, two) jaws. The necessary thickness can be ascertained by using a Dial Indicator or by calculation. If *one* packing is used then the thickness is given by:–

$$T = 1.5E \left[1 - \frac{1}{2}\frac{E}{D} - \frac{3}{8}\left(\frac{E}{D}\right)^3 \right]$$

Where E = required offset
T = packing thickness
D = Dia of work gripped in the jaws.

It is prudent to use a shim right round the machined surface under the jaws, as they may be holding the work by their corners and could mark the surface. The value of 'D' must include twice the shim thickness. This formula will be within one part in 800 – i.e. an error of about 0.0003 in. when E=0.25 inch. This is better than the chuck accuracy, so that use of a dial indicator is needed for final check to take account of chuck error.

Chuck and Center Work
There was a time when the use of the tailstock center in conjunction with a self-centering chuck was disparaged; a relic, no doubt, of the days when normal chuck run-out was far higher than it is today. With work of reasonable length, however, no harm at all can result from supporting the tail end of

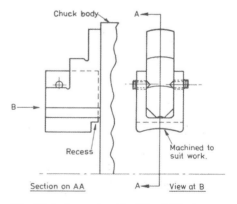

Fig. 89 *An improvised "soft jaw". The jaw must be a good fit on the sides of the hard jaws, and is retained in place by the pointed grub-screws. The jaw is tightened onto a ring set in the recess when machining the profile.*

The Self-centering Chuck 67

the work in this way, and there are many circumstances when it can be a great help. Trouble is often experienced when turning slender workpieces between centers, with chatter especially. If one end is held in the self-centering chuck (or in a properly set-up independent chuck) the work is stiffened, the natural frequency of vibration is altered, and chatter may well disappear. Holding one end in a chuck may enable heavier cuts to be taken when part of the piece has to be roughed down to a much smaller diameter. And, of course, there are cases where it is not easy to fit a conventional carrier dog. I never have any hesitation in using this combination, with one proviso: that it is possible to cut an accurate center in the end of the workpiece.

There are certain limitations. A piece machined entirely in the chuck will be true; a piece machined entirely between centers will be true also; but a piece machined using both may not be. If the chuck is running out by, say, 1½ mil, then the chuck end of the workpiece will 'orbit' by that amount while the tailstock end can rotate only about the lathe centers. Fortunately the error – on the sort of work demanding this treatment – will be very small, but it can be there.

There is a risk that as the work heats up during cutting it will be thrust further into the chuck as it expands. This must be taken care of, and although the 'running center' has certain advantages I prefer to use the ordinary pattern in most cases. This gives a 'witness' of expansion and warns that the tailstock pressure must be eased. The second problem which may arise from the same cause is that feed-dial readings used for locating shoulders – i.e. for dimensions along the length of the work – may be

thrown awry if the work is thrust further into the chuck jaws.

Four- and Six-Jaw Chucks
The virtue of the four-jaw 'concentric' chuck is obvious; it can hold square stock, and model engineers are frequently faced with the job of turning square material for columns and the like. They cost about 50% more than their three-jaw counterparts, and the guaranteed accuracy is about the same. However, the consequences of jaw wear are more serious, as while a worn three-jaw will still grip on all jaws, one with four cannot do. For all that, I find the one I have to be invaluable, despite the wear. (It was bought second hand, and is very old!) Fortunately it is rare that absolute concentricity between the square and the turned part of a workpiece is important.

The purpose of a SIX-jaw chuck may be obscure! It has two main uses. First, for holding soft or easily marked materials. The grip is distributed over twice the area of the work and can be lighter. Second, when holding delicate rings or cylinders. Even the normal six-jaw will introduce less distortion, but the 'watchmaker's' type, which has very wide jaw faces, introduces practically no distortion at all. (See Fig. 55 page 45.) Such chucks are expensive, and hardly worth the cost unless the specialist work needing them is undertaken.

Use and Abuse
The self-centering chuck is very easy to use – that is the point of it! One simply enters the work in the jaws and tightens them with the key. If rings, or solids of large diameters, are being held then it is necessary to tap the work back so that it sits on the flat face of the jaws (which are ground to similar limits as are the

68   WORKHOLDING IN THE LATHE FOR HOME MACHINISTS

radial faces). However, the very fact that the chuck is so easy to use readily leads to its being badly treated.

First, only when unavoidable should work be held in the jaws as shown in Fig. 90. It IS sometimes impossible to avoid when carrying out a second operation on a small workpiece, but should never be necessary when machining raw stock. An extra inch of material to give a good grip may cost another penny or so; a new set of jaws can cost $32. And this practice does lead to irreparable jaw damage unless no more than the very lightest pressure is exerted. The effect is to wear the jaw guides so that they can never again grip full length and if the practice is habitual then the face of the jaws themselves will suffer.

It goes without saying that the chuck key should NEVER be left in the jaws, not for a second. To enforce the habit of taking out the key, fit a spring as shown in Fig. 91. This will expel the key whether you like it or not! The spring should be slightly conical, so that it grips the shank near the handle but is free elsewhere. (I believe that Pratts now supply their keys like this.) It is almost as great a crime, and one which can do equally expensive damage, to apply tubes or other extensions to the chuck key. It is the right length for the job, and if the chuck won't grip, then something else is wrong.

Probably DIRT is the greatest enemy. Self-centering chucks are expensive, and they are complicated. They cost much more than a micrometer, so treat them in the same way! Keep them clean, and make sure that the scroll and the pinions are lubricated from time to time. (I use a heavy Molybdenum-based oil on mine.) 'Precision' chucks usually have an oiling point, and this should be used.

Store chucks with the jaws downwards, so that swarf does not fall into the

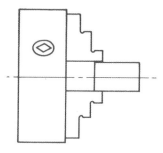

Fig. 90 *Not good practice! Holding a very short workpiece like this puts excessive strain on the jaw guides, as well as being liable to cause wear at the front of the jaw surface.*

mandrel nose fitting. Various devices have been described from time to time to remove swarf and dirt from the fitting threads; the point of a bent scriber is as good a tool as any, but a double one, made up from steel wire is better. Fig. 92. Note the double turn on the 'spring' part. Naturally, the mandrel nose thread must be equally clean and have a trace

Fig. 91 *The safety chuck key.*

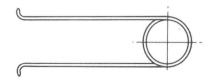

Fig. 92 *Backplate thread-cleaning tool. 3mm BDMS is suitable material.*

of oil on the bedding surfaces. Opinions differ on the wisdom of dismantling chucks to clean the interior. Some people hold that to do so may upset the initial accuracy. However, as we have seen, the runout even on a new chuck is measurable and if the backplate is machined as already suggested, can be put right. I would hesitate to dismantle a Griptru unless it is essential – and as I haven't got one, never have done so! But I do take down all my chucks and clean them periodically. The rule is to put all parts back where they came from and if the pinions, for example, are not marked to their holes put this right. There is no other difficulty and once the chuck has been cleaned and re-oiled you will be surprised how much better it performs!

The point about 'putting things back where they came from' applies, of course, to the jaws of any scroll chuck. They are numbered, and so are the grooves. The drill is to turn the key until the outer end of the scroll just appears in groove No. 1. Turn back till it has just disappeared and then insert the jaw. Pressing this inwards turn the key forwards until the scroll end just appears in groove two, then back slightly and insert jaw No. 2; and so on for jaw

Fig. 93
Removing a tight chuck. Pull the belt by hand!

No. 3. The one thing to avoid is to try to insert the jaw if ANY of the scroll end is showing. To do so may burr the scroll and this will throw concentricity awry.

Never try to remove a stubborn chuck by belting the key with a mallet. Set the machine in back-gear, and with a piece of wood between one jaw and the lathebed pull the belt backwards, Fig. 93. This will loosen the stiffest chuck. As a general rule it may be taken that stiff fitting is a sign of something wrong, usually a tiny piece of swarf in the thread causing it to bind on the nose radius. It follows that a stiff chuck will usually lose its concentricity as well, and immediate attention to the fault is called for.

Self-centering Chuck – Conclusion
The self-centering or concentric chuck provides a convenient means of holding circular or hexagonal work with a reasonable degree of accuracy (or square work if the chuck has four jaws). It is subject to error, which is likely to increase with wear, and for really accurate work the independent chuck should be resorted to. Provided it is reasonably treated, and that the limitations *are* recognized, however, it will give many years of good service. If the chuck is backplate mounted, rather than screwing directly to the mandrel nose it is possible to set it to give a T.I.R. averaging about 0.0015 in. over the whole range of movement of both sets of jaws, with a figure for the 'most common setting' of less than 0.001 inch. I have no hesitation in recommending the independent chuck as the 'first buy' when fitting up a lathe, and always regard it as the 'best buy', but the 'three-jaw' is so convenient and saves so much time that it must come a good second.

CHAPTER 6

Unusual chucks

As I said at the beginning of this book, the number of workholding devices contrived for the lathe over the last couple of hundred years is legion. Most have been replaced by more effective modern types, but some have simply been forgotten, and others disdained because they are not 'up to date'. In this section I hope to bring to your attention a few which 'may come in useful'. It is not, however, my intention to deal with the 'exotics' – Eccentric, Elliptical turning, Uprights, and Rectilinear, to say nothing of the cycloidal and the geometric chuck. These, the common tools of the 'Ornamental' turner, have little place in the model engineer's armory, though I do use my Holtzapffel elliptical chuck to turn oval flanges.

The Bell Chuck
This has already been mentioned and is illustrated on page 41 in two forms (Fig. 50). It has been replaced by the modern four-jaw independent chuck, but does have the advantage that it is small, and in the 8-screw form can not only hold very small diameter work but can also be used to set work of larger size at a small angle. I do not use mine (shown on the right in the photo) very often,

but when I do it is because nothing else will serve. The setting up procedure is the same as for an independent chuck with one difference; the work is first centered roughly using all eight screws, and then *fine* set with the d.t.i. close to the chuck using the front screws only. The indicator is then moved further along the workpiece and the rear set of screws adjusted, the process then being repeated until the desired concentricity – or eccentricity – has been achieved.

The Cup Chuck
This takes many forms, the commonest being seen in Fig. 94. The interior is machined to a very slight cone, so that work driven into it is wedged in place. It finds its greatest use when machining blocks of wood, plastic, or similar soft material. If held in the modern chuck the material is indented by the jaws and after a time these lose their grip. With a cup chuck it is only necessary to rough shape the wood with an axe (or turn it using the four-jaw if you are unskilled with the axe!) and then drive it into the cup. Provided the wood is not wet (and hence liable to shrink when dry) it will not come loose. An advantage not to be

Unusual chucks 71

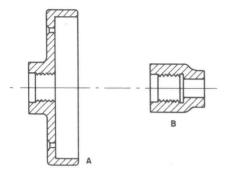

Fig. 94 *Proportions of large (A) and small (B) cup-chucks. Note the wood-screw holes in (A), useful when a softwood block is to be held for any length of time.*

dismissed is that the body of the chuck is very little larger than the work – it may even be smaller – unlike that of the four-jaw independent which might be the alternative. I have a number of these, all made to fit the Holtzapffel, but which can be held in the self centering chuck by the boss when needed on the Myford. Fig. 95 shows a number of them, all of brass, though I do have a few in iron or steel as well.

A useful variation is the wax cup chuck (made of boxwood) or the solder cup chuck (of brass or steel). Both work in the same way. They resemble the cup chuck, but are shallower, and are used to hold irregularly shaped workpieces. The piece is set in the cavity, and adjusted more or less to the correct position, where it may either be wedged temporarily or held with clamps. Wax (or plumber's solder, as the case may be) is then poured into the cavity and will be found to hold the work securely. I have also used Wood's Metal, which melts at below boiling water temperature, when holding (e.g.) part of a diecast toy needing repair. Another interesting example was the machining of the handles of the plugs of a number of model drain cocks. These, commercially made, had taper handles, but I needed them to be covered with horn. The plug element was set in a small cup with sealing wax, with the handle set as vertical as might be. The cup was then held in an 8-screw bell chuck, which enabled me to set the handle both central and truly upright for turning down.

The Master-and-Slave Chuck

This is a very useful accessory indeed, but seems to have been totally for-

Fig. 95 *A group of brass cup-chucks.*

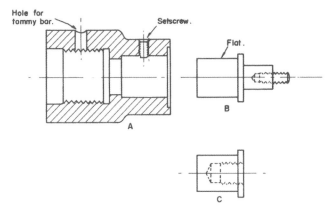

Fig. 96 *The Master and Slave chuck. (A) is the master, and (B) & (C) two typical slaves. Note the tommy-bar hole in (A) used when removing it from the mandrel nose.*

gotten. Fig. 96 shows the arrangement. Normally made to screw onto the mandrel nose it can also be arranged to fit the mandrel nose taper, but in that case a drawbar is essential. The hole in the master-chuck is accurately bored to a standard diameter, and has (as a rule) a smaller hole bored right through. The 'Slave' is made to suit the work in hand – it may be a screwed socket to accept a union body, a short mandrel, or any fixture you please. The shank is a close fit in the bored socket and has a flat to engage the grub-screw. I usually make a shoulder to bed down on the face of the Master. The Slave will thus always be concentric and set exactly to length every time it is used – far more accurate than using a similar device set in the self-centering chuck even if it is marked 'to No. 1 Jaw' in the classical fashion. There is a further use, too. On the odd occasion it happens that work set in the normal headstock center is too close *to* the headstock. True, you may have a 'Long center' just for this eventuality, but the Master chuck will serve instead – the 'Slave' is simply a steel center. I need not go into detail on the various slaves which can be made up but it is,

perhaps, worth mentioning that the master chuck is far better for holding slot drills than is the normal self-centering chuck. The inherent error in the latter will always cause such a cutter to cut large, but a carefully made master chuck will hold it dead true. (The well-known Autolock FC3 'Throwaway' cutters are normally held in such a master, but of the type which is set in the mandrel nose taper).

The body may be made of steel; though cast iron is kinder to the mandrel nose there is just a risk of stripping the thread for the set screw. The size depends upon the class of work normally done in the shop, but if the bore is 0.75 in dia. by 1 in. long this will meet most needs. The machining of the register and thread to suit the lathe is done in the same fashion as when machining a chuck back plate – a good fit to the register and face, but not too tight on the thread. (I bore the threaded part to a diameter about 0.25 times the pitch less than the diameter of the screw; this ensures that binding on the crest of the thread cannot occur). After ensuring that the face does bed properly on the shoulder of the lathe

Unusual chucks 73

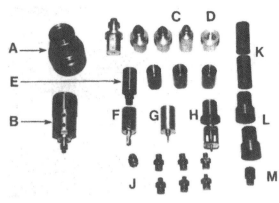

Fig. 97 Part of the author's Master-and-Slave chuck system. A. The master chuck for Myford lathe. B. Master for the Lorch machine, with one of the plain arbors (C) fitted. Slaves fit both masters. C. Four plain arbors, with cap washers and setscrews. D. Arbor for machining eccentrics, made up specially when 12 identicasl eccentrics were required. E. Double-ended female thread slaves, one of which carries a male adapter, J. F. Slave adapter to carry FC3 or other endmills having ¼ inch shanks. G. Center-setting point, for setting up work on the vertical slide. H. Lantern chuck. Several different sized lanterns can be fitted to the same screw. J. Male thread adapters. All have ⅜ × 26 bases to fit one of the female arbors seen at E, and each carries a female BA thread as well as the male thread at the working end. K. Plain blank slaves, made from ¾ inch ground mild steel stock. L. Stepped blanks, with 1 inch diameter heads. M. Blank for type J, ready threaded one end to ⅜ × 26 tpi. Most of the components have been heat-blued as a precaution against rust in storage.

mandrel, the 'business end' is machined with the Master screwed onto the mandrel nose. Note the recess on the end in Fig. 96 – this reduces the risk of burring the edge of the bore. The setscrew need not be large – 3⁄16 in. BSF or M5 will be adequate – but it should be of a length which just does *not* project from the surface when tightened. The 'Slaves' are, of course, made up to suit the job in hand, and can be of any material you please. The flat to engage the setscrew is an imperative, for without it burrs will develop and accuracy will suffer – or you may even find that you can't get it out! Bushes can, of course, be used should it be necessary to hold a slave or a workpiece smaller than the bored hole but, if used, should have a hole through for the setscrew, so that the latter bears on the part that matters. The loss of accuracy is slight.

The device is incredibly useful and it is surprising that it has been forgotten for so long. The latest mention I have been able to find is in a book on lathe work by Percival Marshall, published in the days when *Model Engineer* cost about three cents! (0.8p new money!) Fig. 97 shows part of my own outfit, the 'slaves' being interchangeable to 'masters' on three lathes.

The Lantern Chuck

No, not to hold lanterns, but so named because it can, in one form, look like one! Its purpose (Fig. 98) is to hold small headed components while machining the shank. I suppose that everyone has experienced the frustration of trying to hold a small screw by the head in the normal chuck, and the Lantern provides the alternative. Usually found with an 8mm collet arbor, but I have several which fit the master chuck previously mentioned. They are not intended for large work – which can, in any case, usually be held in the self-centering chuck – but rather for reforming the ends of screws which have been shortened, and similar work. The hole in the lantern is *not* tapped, so that plain work can be held if need be.

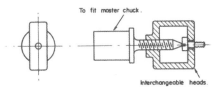

Fig. 98 *A lantern-chuck for use with Fig. 96.*

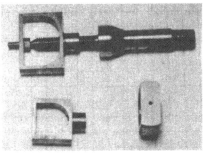

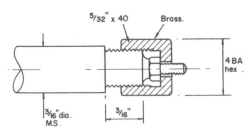

Fig. 99 *Lantern chuck on 8mm colletarbor, seen holding a 7BA bolt. Below are two alternative heads, with smaller holes.*

Fig. 100 *(left). A lantern chuck as used to face the ends of 16BA bolts or studs. The cap could be knurled if desired, rather than hexagon.*

The set on my Boley has three interchangeable lanterns, covering the range from about 7BA down to 12BA, and I also have a very small one for 16BA. This one (Fig. 100) has no apertures in the side of the lantern so that the cap must be removed to change workpieces, but I judged that the extra time here would be less than that needed to make the apertures in the side of the cap. The device can be used to hold studs if a nut is screwed on the stud end first. It should be noted that is not a *precise* chuck; there is bound to be a small clearance in the hole. But it does serve its purpose and holds small screws with no risk of damage to the head. If the screw is inserted head outwards, with a nut inside the lantern, it makes the polishing of screw-heads an easy job.

Wood Block Chucks

I have already mentioned the use of a wooden block attached to the faceplate, but wood blocks screwed onto the mandrel nose are equally useful. The 'Ornamental' turner regards them as standard, and their use is not to be disdained. They provide a useful method of holding delicate work with-out distortion. We have already seen that no chuck of the conventional type can hold work without causing a deflection – even a six-jaw bezel chuck will set up distortion if not carefully used. But work set on a spigot, or in a recess machined on a wood block, and held thereto with glue, double-sided tape, or (if convenient) woodscrews, can be held with much reduced risk. The common objection is that 'You can't take a decent cut'. 'It all depends on what you mean by Decent'! Some time ago I read a description – I think of a new type of cutter – where the writer explained that he couldn't load it fully as the machine had no more than 120 h.p. available at the machine spindle! Horses for courses – a 'decent' cut is one which removes metal at a rate which strains neither the work, the tool, nor the machine, and if the workpiece fixing is the limiting factor one must adjust depths of cut to suit.

There is no problem machining blocks of Boxwood or Lignum Vitae to suit any type of lathe mandrel, and as the block is usually machined on the face to suit each individual application extreme accuracy of fit is not essential. However, if the turner already has a cup chuck the wood block can be set in this and then almost any piece of hardwood will serve. I have, in fact, used boxwood 'slaves' in a master chuck before now. And some years ago rechamfered half-a-dozen brass nuts when screwed onto a wooden dowel! Once the use of wood is accepted as 'normal' it is just a case of using the most suitable material for the work in hand, wood, metal, or anything else. The main problem for many is the setting of woodscrews in Box or Lignum. These are tough materials – Lignum has an ultimate strength of 11 tons/sq. in. – and some modern woodscrews seem to be made of metallized putty. The trick is to drill a tapping hole (not forgetting to enlarge it at the top if the shank of the screw may enter) and then tap it out. I have a number of good woodscrews, gauges 8, 10 and 12, which I have first gashed, as on a tap, and then casehardened. By using the appropriate 'tap', not to full depth, the insertion of the ordinary screw is relatively easy.

I have already remarked on the use of tape and 'Turner's Cement' in the section on faceplate work. Fig. 101 shows a wood block in use as a wax chuck. The irregular piece of ivory, sawn from the side of the hollow part of a tusk, is to be machined to a flat slab. The cavity in the wood block has been machined flat and enlarged as need be with a chisel. The flat side of the piece has been set in the cavity and plain candlewax poured in.

Fig. 102 shows machining in progress, the cuts being about $\frac{1}{32}$ in. deep at each pass. No trouble was experienced, and after facing the outer side the piece was reversed to machine the sawn face.

Fig. 101 *A fragment of ivory held in a woodblock chuck with candlewax.*

Fig. 102 *The ivory in process of machining. $\frac{1}{32}$ inch cuts were taken without slippage.*

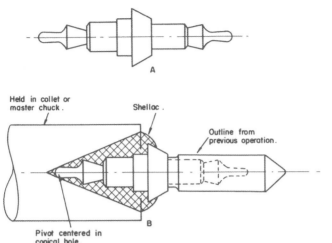

Fig. 103 Top. Typical shape of a balance-wheel staff, which might be 12 or 15mm long. Below. The partially machined workpiece held in a conical chuck with shellac. The workpiece material is hardened and tempered carbon steel.

There are many other chucks or holding devices which may be classed as 'unusual' but space won't permit dealing with even a tenth of them. The model engineer has become so accustomed to his self-centering three-jaw and the independent four-jaw (with an occasional, tentative, recourse to turning between centers) that alternatives are seldom considered. So, as a tailpiece, I show Fig. 103 which shows one method of machining a watch balance-wheel staff (spindle). These are made of high carbon steel, hardened and tempered to blue; tough stuff to turn by any standard. After machining one end held in a normal collet the work is reversed and held in the conical cavity shown using a *small globule of melted shellac*. After centering (using the simple methods of the watchmaker, which need not concern us) the material (about 54 Rockwell hardness, and perhaps of 100 ton/sq. in. tensile strength) is turned to shape with a hand graver. A different class of work from ours, no doubt – you need a magnifying glass for one thing – but nevertheless shows what can be done with no more than a piece of hole and a blob of wax!

CHAPTER 7

Collets

The collet, or split chuck, is a development from the wood-spring chuck used by ornamental turners for several hundred years. Seen in Fig. 104, this comprises a block of Box or similar hardwood bored out to form a cavity of depth about equal to its diameter, and the exterior machined to a slight taper. The walls of the cavity are slit and a ring of wood or metal will, when driven onto the taper, close the walls of the chuck onto the workpiece.

Fig. 104 *A wood spring chuck, made by the author for his Holtzapffel lathe.*

The turner would have a range of sizes (I have about a dozen) but the chuck can easily be rebored to suit any special size or, to hold short work, have a step turned in the bore against which the workpiece can be located. Once the walls became too thin to hold securely, the chuck is discarded and a new one made; the walls are thick enough to allow this. (I have one 4 in. diameter dating from 1847, unused so far, with walls ⅝ in. thick.)

In the modern collet the same principle is applied, but as a rule the taper is formed in the lathe mandrel and the workholding part of the chuck either drawn into or driven onto it using drawbars, closing rings, or similar devices. There are many variations, some of which I will deal with later, but Figs 105 & 106 shows the two types most commonly found in small lathes. Fig. 105 is the well-known 'Draw-in' type, in which the collet is drawn back by the screwed drawbar to close the nose onto the workpiece. The collet may have an internal thread on the tail, but is usually external, as shown. Fig. 106 is the so-called 'dead-length' collet; here the nose is closed by a screwed ring pressing a closing piece onto the

Fig. 105 The "Draw-in" type of collet.

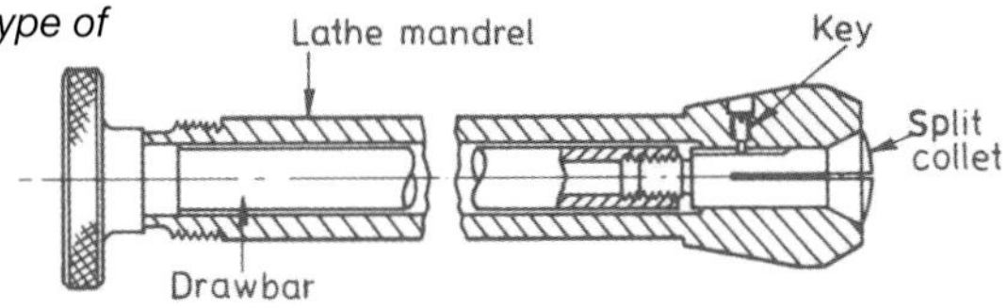

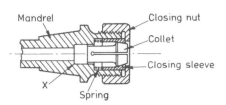

external taper at the collet nose. The collet itself beds back onto a shoulder at the point 'X'. This ensures that the nose of the collet always projects the same amount from the lathe mandrel, whereas with the draw-in type there can be a slight variation. The principles involved are the same for both types, and as the dead-length type is rarely found and even more rarely needed for our class of work I will concentrate on the almost universal draw-in type.

Fig. 106 The "Dead Length" collet. This type is usually operated by power closing systems, but a manual nut has been shown for clarity.

Draw-in Collets

The size of the collet is designated by two figures. First, the size of the shank, 'A' in Fig. 108. This can range from 6mm for small watchmaker's lathes up to 30mm, with 8mm and 10mm being the most usual in our class of work. So, an '8mm collet' is one which is 8mm dia. on the body. The size of the work aperture, 'd', is usually quoted in tenths of millimeters, a 'No 8' being 0.8mm dia. and 'No. 40' 4.0mm dia., but both fractional and decimal inch sizes may be found occasionally, especially on George Adams' machines. This diameter, if quoted as 'through chuck', will be the largest size of rod which can be passed right through. However, the 'largest bore' means that which a collet of body diameter 'A' can hold, the nose being bored as seen in the inset detail in Fig. 108. For an 8mm size collet the two figures are, typically, 4½mm and 7.0mm, and 6mm/8mm for one with 10mm dia. shank. The smallest size I

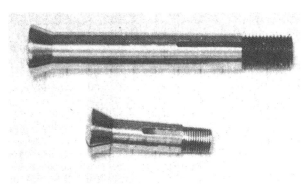

Fig. 107 Above; a 10mm collet from a LORCH precision lathe. Below; an 8mm Wolff-Jahn collet.

Collets 79

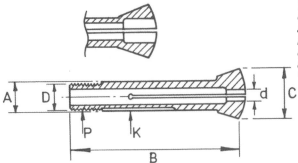

Fig. 108 *Leading dimensions of a draw-in collet – these are defined in the text. The inset shows the end of a collet in which the work diameter is greater than the "right through" dimension.*

have in 8mm collets takes work 0.2mm dia., and as a rule the diameter 'd' rises in increments of 0.1mm up to about 4mm, after which it may go up by 0.2mm steps; this varies with different makes. For larger collets the steps are usually at 0.5mm intervals above, say, 7.5mm bore.

The other important dimensions indicated on the sketch are: *Head diameter, 'C'* Slight differences do not matter, but if 'C' is much smaller or larger than standard the taper may not bed properly. Most 8mm collets are around 12.5mm, but those by Adams are only 10.7mm diameter. *Body Length, 'B'* There is usually a sufficient tolerance on the length of the drawbar to accommodate small changes here, but in the particular case of 15mm dia. collets there were two common sizes – 44mm and 72mm – and these clearly are not interchangeable, so that a separate drawbar is needed for each.

Thread diameter 'D' and Pitch, 'P' These do vary in diameter, pitch, and thread form even though the shank diameter 'A' may be the same. A full list is given in the *Model Engineer's Handbook* for 8mm collets. The main point to note is that though the two common pitches on 8mm collets (40 t.p.i. and 0.625mm) are almost identical the thread form is different, the former being 55 deg. Whitworth shape and the latter 60 deg. metric. It IS possible, with a slack drawbar, to accommodate both, but only if care is used not to overtighten. Even more care must be taken with Geo. Adams 10mm collets, as these have a buttress thread.

Keyway, K. This is the dimension which usually prevents complete interchangeability of collets of the same nominal diameter. The purpose of the key is to prevent the collet body from rotating when the drawbar is tightened – it is not a driver key. Each lathe-maker seems to use a different width and projection, and if an attempt is made to use a collet with a small keyway in a lathe with a larger size key irreparable damage can be done to both. However, it is possible to alter the keyways if the number of odd collets justifies this and I described a method in my book *Simple Workshop Devices*, by Argus Books Ltd. There is no harm in using an *oversize* keyway.

Cone Angle §, I shall have more to say about this in a moment, but for the present it should be noted that the most common figure is 40 deg., though this is by no means universal. If faced with a CHOICE of collets, anything much less than 30 deg. may exert too great a

80 WORKHOLDING IN THE LATHE FOR HOME MACHINISTS

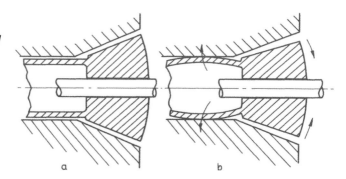

Fig. 109 *Diagram showing (exaggerated) the effect of the closing forces on the collet body and head. At (a), touching the work but not drawn back, (b) After tightening the drawbar.*

pressure on the workpiece, while angles of 60 deg. or more may need excessive drawbar pull. (The situation is different on 'Production' class lathes, where the collets are operated by cams or air cylinders). Note that some lathe and collet manufacturers quote the *half-angle* – their 20 deg. will be § = 40 deg. in Fig. 108.

Workholding in a Collet

We have already noted that the collet is closed by the backward pull of the drawbar and the wedging action of the taper. The collet itself is of hardened and tempered steel and so manufactured that it will spring open when the drawbar is slackened. This means that the wall of the collet body must be relatively thin – perhaps 1½mm for an 8mm collet. Even though the work-aperture is accurately sized there will be a slight backward movement of the collet as it grips. This means that the relative angle of collet and holder will change. See Fig. 109. To allow for this the manufacturers of the lathe will have applied a correction to the angle of the socket in the mandrel. This is small – on my 10mm Lorch the socket angle is 39¼ deg. as near as I can measure, but this may vary from make to make. The effect is that when work of the correct diameter is gripped the taper beds over the full area. The walls of the collet body have flexed a trifle, and, of course, there is slight deflection both of work and collet under the influence of the gripping forces.

Consider now the effect when a workpiece slightly oversize is gripped. Fig. 110. The contact between work and collet is at 'Y', but that between collet and mandrel is at 'X'. There is a considerable bending force and, in addition, magnification of the gripping effort owing to the small area of contact at 'Y'. The result is twofold. First, the grip will be insecure, there being a

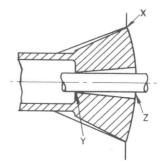

Fig. 110 *Collet asked to hold an oversize workpiece. Accuracy will suffer, as it is not firmly gripped at Z, and it may mark the surface at Y.*

Collets 81

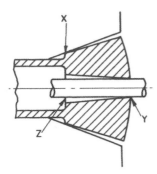

Fig. 111 *Collet asked to hold work which is undersize. Clearance at Z results in insecure grip and loss of accuracy.*

ground silver steel is closer (+0.000mm to −0.010mm) so that this may not be so serious, but **you must not be surprised if you find that both accuracy and repeatability are poor when holding 'B.D.M.S.',** especially in the smaller sizes. (In passing, it is worth noting that the smaller the cone angle the greater will be the effect.) The lesson for us is that when doing work which demands the accuracy provided by a collet workholder we should use ground stock – either mild steel or silver steel – or, if none is available, carry out a preliminary sizing operation from larger stock. The problem is acute when attempting to hold inch size material in metric collets or vice versa. Comparing the usual metric equivalents with the nearest standard sizes of 8mm collet the errors are as under:-

Stock dia.	Collet size mm	error in.
1/16	1.6	0.0008
3/32	2.4	0.0008
1/8	3.2	0.001
5/32	4.0	0.0012
3/16	4.8	0.0015
7/32	5.6	0.0016
1/4	6.4	0.002

clearance (albeit, perhaps, a small one) at 'Z'; and, second, the collet will tend to mark the work. The same consideration applies if undersize work is gripped, as shown in Fig. 111. The positions of the points 'X', 'Y' and 'Z' have changed, that is all. In either case *the concentricity is bound to suffer.*

This second case is the more usual when we are machining from barstock. For obvious reasons bright drawn steel has an 'undersize' tolerance and may be as much as a couple of mil down on the nominal size. The tolerance on

The collet is rightly considered as the most accurate of the chucking-type workholders, but it can be no more 'accurate' than the work it is holding. To expect a collet to give perfect repeatability on bright drawn steel (or, worse, brass) which is neither true to dimension nor perfectly round is asking too much.

It is perhaps, worth mentioning that several designs of collets have been devised to overcome this problem; obviously production machines, especially automatics or N.C. type, are not limited to using ground stock! One approach is that of the 'double taper'

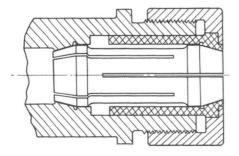

Fig. 112 *Principle of the double-taper collet, which can hold work slightly under- or oversize. The dosing arrangements are diagrammatic only.*

collet, shown diagrammatically in Fig. 112. It has a closing cone at both ends, and both ends are split, with the slits running alternately. This will accommodate variations from the nominal diameter, for though it cannot grip full length it does hold the work at two points far enough apart to overcome the problem we have been discussing. A similar approach is found in the Schaublin collet, one type of which is shown in Fig. 113. It was introduced as a toolholder – for parallel shank cutters – but I understand that it has been applied to workholding as well. It will accommodate variations of the order of ±0.5mm on sizes over 4mm dia., but requires fairly heavy closing pressure and there is some tendency to mark unhardened work.

Before going on to consider other matters a few hints on the use of the most common type of collet (Fig. 107) may not be out of place.

(1) Make sure that the collet fits the lathe. Some may be marked with a symbol, two letter 'C' back to back; these are made by Crawford Collets Ltd, Witney, Oxfordshire, and bear a serial number by which they may be identified.
(2) If the collet 'doesn't want to go in' the keyway is probably undersize; check this with a collet of known provenance.
(3) Lubricate the outside of the collet and the thread with thin machine oil; I use Tellus 11.
(4) Take the greatest care that both mandrel and collet are perfectly clean before fitting. After use both wash out and blow out the hole and especially the slits in the collet, as dirt can collect there. Oil well before putting away.

Fig. 113 *A Schaublin collet.*

(5) Use the minimum drawbar force which will hold the work. If it needs great force, then either (a) the stock is the wrong size for the collet, (b) the key is binding, (c) the collet is over long (or there is dirt in the drawbar thread) so that it is not pulling up properly, (d) there is dirt in the slits of the collet.
(6) *Select* the stock you use with collets – run the micrometer over it and set aside that which is closest to size. Use metric stock in metric collets and vice versa. Always clean stock before using it.
(7) Do not use the collets 'just because you have them' Reserve them for work which justifies them – they are precision tools for use on precision work.
(8) NEVER overtighten the drawbar. If more than light handgrip is needed, something is wrong – at least so far as 6, 8, or 10mm collets are concerned.

Stepped Collets

Fig. 114 shows an external step chuck fitted to the Boley watchmaker's lathe. The steps are at 2mm intervals on the diameter and it will be appreciated that

Fig. 114 *An 8mm step-chuck collet, on a small Boley watchmaker's lathe.*

25mm internal work diameter in steps of 0.4mm. A similar set of five chucks has internal steps, covering discs from 5.6mm up to 23.2m these being closed by the normal internal taper in the mandrel bore. Fig. 115 shows such an internal chuck, with 8 steps, but in this case on the larger Lorch lathe. These take from 6mm up to something over 40mm diameter in 40 steps and are too large to be controlled by tapers on the mandrel nose itself. Closing pieces are used instead, screwed onto the mandrel. (This machine is arranged both with a collet bore and a screwed nose, the

in this case the collet must *expand* to grip the work. The lathe mandrel is made with an external taper to allow this, in addition to the internal one. There are five such collets to a set, and each has the array of six steps 0.4mm larger in diameter than the next. The full set, therefore, covers 30 diameters from 11.4mm up to

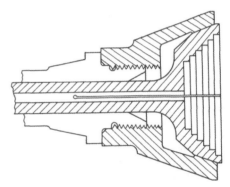

Fig. 115 *A 10mm internal step-chuck on a Lorch precision lathe. The largest work held is 40mm diameter.*

Fig. 116 *Closing piece screwed onto the mandrel nose, for the step chuck seen in Fig. 115.*

latter taking chucks in the usual way.) Fig. 116 shows the arrangement.

This type of collet is invaluable. The most delicate ring can be held without undue distortion, and the grip is adequate – obviously one does not take heavy cuts when machining such workpieces. The repeatability is not as good as that achieved with the ordinary split collet, but is well within the limits needed for most model engineering applications. The remarks on the use of

84 WORKHOLDING IN THE LATHE FOR HOME MACHINISTS

normal collets apply, but owing to the many sharp corners cleaning can be rather difficult. An old toothbrush and clean paraffin form an essential accessory!

The Button Collet
This may be met with if a second-hand set of watchmaker's equipment has been purchased – Fig. 117. These are intended for holding the winding buttons of pocket-watches while remachining the stems. They are usually in sets of ten, with diameters from 5 up to 14mm, but few watchmakers would have a complete set. Their use is somewhat limited, but they are handy for holding, e.g., bronze balls while drilling.

Brass Auxiliary Chucks
These are no more than small brass split collets, with no drawbar thread, usually 5mm outside diameter (though they can be found larger) and run from about 0.2mm up to about 3mm diameter in the bore. Their function is to hold delicate screw threads which would be damaged by the hard steel collet. They are simply inserted in the standard 5mm (No. 50) collet and when the drawbar is pulled up the larger steel collet tightens the small brass one. Such collets can easily be made – they need no taper, just a shoulder to butt against the face of the steel collet – and if made with a *threaded* hole will secure small screws with no damage and with the certainty of running true.

Solid Collet Arbors
Many devices can be held in the mandrel of a lathe equipped for collets – Fig. 118 is one example, and perhaps the small drill chuck is another obvious one. One important point must be kept in mind when making any such – the angle of the taper

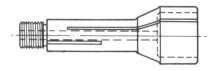

Fig. 117 *A watchmaker's "Button Chuck". It will hold work larger than the normal collet.*

in this case must *coincide* with that on the mandrel nose. There is no 'correction' needed here as there is for the closing of a split collet. Care must be taken over this if the arbor is to seat properly. Some

Fig. 118 *A small milling cutter fitted to an 8mm arbor.*

machines have the correction applied to the mandrel taper; others (Geo. Adams is one) applied it to the angle of the collet itself. To make such arbors it is, therefore, necessary first to make a gauge

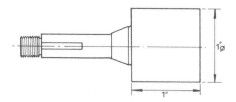

Fig. 119 *Type of blank arbor made up by the author, for subsequent machining to suit the work in hand.*

Collets 85

which must be matched with marking blue to the machine and then make a female gauge from this to use when machining the arbor. For this reason it is worth making a number of blank arbors (Fig. 119 is typical of mine, for an 8mm lathe) which can then be machined to their final shape when needed. If there is to be any error on the taper at all it should be such that the arbor bears more at the larger end of the taper than at the smaller.

Collet Adapters

6mm and 8mm collets are coming onto the market second-hand in increasing numbers as we enter the era of 'throwaway' electronic watches, which cannot, as a rule, be repaired and which don't need lathes even when they can. The larger 10mm collets are less often met with. However, it is a bit frustrating if a set of such collets is knocked down to you for a song at the local sale and then you find that your lathe has a No.1 or No.2 M.T. taper! There are two usual approaches. One is to make an adapter to screw onto the mandrel nose, and the other an adapter which fits into the Morse socket. The first will permit the use of 10mm (or even larger) collets, but the latter is usually limited to 6mm and 8mm sizes. The screw-on type is made just like the master chuck shown in Fig. 96 page 73, but bored to suit the collet. A drawbar is needed to reach to the rear of the mandrel to effect the closure. (Note that you may have to work with the change-wheel guard open, as if the drawbar passes through this it will prevent access to the change-wheels.) The Morse taper type is shown in Fig. 120, and is made from a No.2 M.T. drill-chuck arbor. Note that in this case the drawbar shoulder beds on the end of the adapter, not on the tail of the lathe mandrel. I give full details for its manufacture in *Simple Workshop Devices* (by Argus Books Ltd.) but the construction is fairly clear from Fig. 120. I use an identical device for holding milling cutters though in that one there is no drawbar – the cutter (on an 8mm arbor like Fig. 118) is set in the arbor

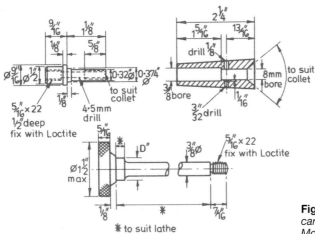

Fig. 120 *An adapter to carry 8mm collets in No. 2 Morse taper sockets.*

86 WORKHOLDING IN THE LATHE FOR HOME MACHINISTS

Fig. 121 *Adapter to carry 8mm collets in the author's ¾ inch master chucks.*

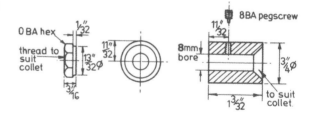

and the closing nut tightened before fitting into the lathe mandrel.

There is a further alternative, and one which I tend to favor. This is shown in Fig. 121. It is a simple adapter to make and fits my Masterchuck. As I have such a chuck for several lathes, all bored to the same diameter (0.750 inch), I can use this where I please. True, the 'Slave' has to be removed from the Master in order to get at the closing nut, but that doesn't take much time.

Length Stops

In semi-production work, where a number of parts of the same dimensions are to be made, it is a great help to have means of setting the work in the collet in the same axial position. This can be effected by using a length stop as shown in Fig. 122. It is a standard accessory for all but the tiny 6mm dia. collets, sometimes listed as an 'Inside Stop'. The stop rod 'A' is gripped by the inner split collet 'B' when the nut 'C' is tightened. This also expands the second split bush 'D' so that it grips the inside of the main collet. It is, of course, necessary to adjust the whole before the collet is set in the lathe, as it is inaccessible inside the drawbar in service. It is easily made, the taper of the cone being about 10 deg. but care must be taken that the outside diameter of the knurled nut 'C' can pass inside the thread of the drawbar.

Larger Collets

The main problem with collets so far described is that the size of stock accepted is limited, and in many cases they cannot hold work 'right through'. The Myford collet system takes barstock up to ½ inch (12.5mm) and can pass up to this size right through the mandrel. (With a special attachment it can also be used as a 'bar feed', operated with the machine running). The closing taper is the No.2 Morse Taper of the mandrel nose itself, and operation is effected by means of a screwed ring fitting the mandrel nose

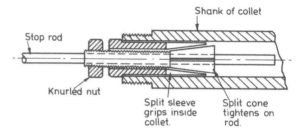

Fig. 122 *Length stop for use with draw-in collets. The nut and head of the screwed member must be small enough to pass inside the drawbar.*

Fig. 123 *The Myford No. 2 MT type collet with its closing ring-nut.*

thread which presses the collet backwards. A special tool, part of the outfit, is used to fit this ring to a recess in the nose of the collet so that it also acts as an extractor.

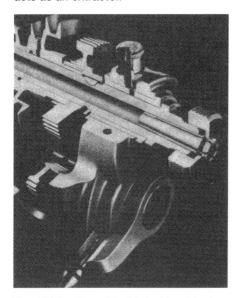

Fig. 124 *Section of the Myford headstock with collet and closing ring in place.*

Fig. 123 shows a collet with its closing ring, and Fig. 124 shows a section of the headstock with all in place. The very small overhang compared with that from a chuck is immediately apparent. A complete outfit with 16 collets, closing ring and fitting tool is seen in Fig. 125.

Collets are available from $1/16$ in. dia. upwards at intervals of $1/64$ in., or the equivalent metric sizes. It is a neat solution, but there are two snags, already hinted at. The taper is very fierce, so that if used on under- or oversized stock marking of the work is almost unavoidable. And this type of collet can only be as accurate as the bore of No.2 M.T. socket – typically 0.001 to 0.002 in/foot.

There is a further Myford type, in which an adapter is screwed onto the mandrel nose and made to accept 'dead length' collets up to $5/8$ in. diameter. A 'Home Made' device of this type was described by Lawrence Sparey some 35 years ago in his book *The Amateur's Lathe* and is available from the M.A.P. Plans Service as drawing number MM 136. (Fig. 126). The limitation here is that unless you have both a proper heat treatment furnace and cylindrical grinding machine the collets must of necessity be soft and will lack 'spring'. If you do set out to make such an outfit remember to apply the small 'angle correction' already referred to. I suggest a difference of 0.75 degrees.

Collets – Summing up
The major virtue of the collet is its inherent accuracy; its major drawback is the extremely limited range it will hold – a tolerance of +0.000 in. to -0.00075 in. for diameters of 0.3 in. and below if repeatability and accuracy is to be maintained. Work can be machined

to within a few mil of the collet face with most types, and incredibly delicate work can be done given sharp tools. The inertia of the rotating mandrel is reduced a great deal compared with when using any type of chuck. It is possible confidently to remove work from a collet and replace it again with negligible loss of concentricity (subject to the tolerance on the stock itself if not a machined surface) and, if need be, to transfer work from one collet-lathe to another. The accuracy and repeatability is only exceeded by working between centers.

However, the limitation mentioned above does have serious consequences. There are no 'standard sizes' in model engineering, and to cover the sizes of work we do needs a complete range of collets, and at close intervals, too. The incremental step of 0.1mm will scarcely cover the range of sizes from one collet to another, so that to cover from 1/32 in. up to 1/4 in. we should need no fewer than 60 collets!

If the class of work you do is such that collets are needed, then they are worth their weight in gold (cost almost that, too) and if you make a good deal of your parts from just a few sizes of stock, then the few collets needed will pay their way. Otherwise, I think not. I confess that though I have something like 120 8mm collets for the little Boley I tend to do most of the work in the chuck; and of the 30 odd 10mm size for the Lorch I use about half a dozen. My 'Collet Adapters' are very seldom used for workholding; their principal job is holding little cutters, slitting saws and, occasionally, the lantern chucks. The collet devices I DO use a great deal are the sets of step-chucks; these I find

Fig. 125 *Myford No. 2 MT collets in case, with the dosing rings in the center-front.*

invaluable and I wouldn't be without them, but for the rest – they come in useful at times, but I doubt if I would miss them all that much if I hadn't got them already.

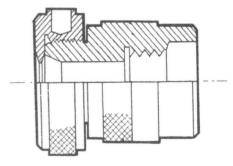

Fig. 126 *The Sparey collet design for Myford lathes. The adapter screws onto the mandrel nose. Though "front closed" the collets are not of the "dead length" type. (From "The Amateur's Lathe, L.H. Sparey)*

CHAPTER 8

Work Steady Rests

The work steady rest can range from a complicated frame carrying slides, springs, rollers and adjusting screws to a chunk of wood or even the odd finger. Before dealing with even part of this great variety let us first have a look at what the steady rest has to do, and why it is necessary.

In applying the tool to the work a force must be applied so that the tool point remains immersed in the workpiece. The direction of this force will depend on the shape of the tool in plan, the front and side rake, and the depth of the cut, and its magnitude depends on the feed-rate, depth of cut, rake angle, and the material being machined. In general, however, the force on the tool will point at an angle downwards, backwards, and away from the headstock. 'When the horse pulls the cart, the cart pulls the horse', or so the horse believes. Or, to be technical, 'Action and reaction are equal and opposite'; if there is a force on the tool there must be an equal and opposite force on the workpiece, and this will lie in exactly the opposite direction to that on the tool – upwards, towards the back of the lathe, and towards the headstock.

This slantendicular force can be 'resolved' into three forces at right angles to each other, as shown in Fig. 127. 'V' is the upward, vertical component; 'Hb' the backward horizontal one; and 'Ha' the axial horizontal component. Equal and opposite forces are felt by the tool point. For a given rate of feed, rake angle, and depth of cut 'V' will not vary much whatever plan form of tool we use, but Ha and Hb are greatly affected. With a knife tool, for example, Hb will be very low indeed, and Ha large, but with a large radius round-nose tool Ha tends to be small and Hb large. If such a tool be even slightly blunt, then Hb can become very large even with light cuts. (With a blunt knife tool, Ha will be large.)

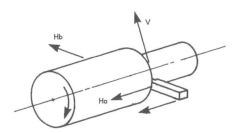

Fig. 127 *Forces experienced by the workpiece under the influence of the cutting tool. Tool moving from right to left.*

Fig. 128 *(a) Deflection will be large at (2) and small at (1). (b) Deflection is large at (2), small at (1) and (3). Note that (2) may not be in the center of the workpiece – see text.*

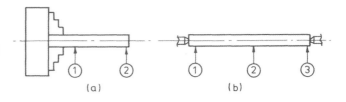

The magnitude of these forces need not concern us, except to remark that it is good practice to keep them small – e.g. by keeping tools sharp. But the very fact that they are there at all is important. For, if we impose a force on a workpiece there is *bound* to be a deflection; the 'immovable post' just cannot exist. This means that the work will bend away from the tool, by an amount which depends on how great the forces are. For a given force the amount of the deflection will depend on the stiffness of the work and the workholder, and, in most cases, on where the forces are applied to the workpiece in relation to its support. Fig. 128. At 'a' we have work held in a chuck or collet; the deflection will be least at (1) and greatest at (2). At 'b' we have work between centers, and we find the deflection least at (1) and (3), and greatest at (2). However, in the latter case the point of greatest deflection need not necessarily be at the center if the work is taper, or has steps on the diameter. Further, if the work is held in a chuck at the headstock end and in a center at the other there will be zero – or a very small – deflection at point (1).

Clearly, from the tool in varying amounts along its length we cannot hope to get the work turned to a uniform size. One reason for using the steady rest is to prevent this from happening. In effect, we provide a support behind the work which exerts forces equal and opposite to those at 'V' and 'Hb'. Yes, I know that this ignores the axial force 'Ha', but the cases where this becomes important are very rare indeed and most of these affect only the lathe mandrel thrust bearing. So, a steady rest may be necessary to prevent work deflection so that we can turn parallel. But there is more to it than that.

Chatter

In Fig. 129 (a) is shown a tool taking a cut of depth 'd', and as a result the forces V and H are applied to the workpiece. These forces cause the work to deflect, as shown at (b), reducing the depth of cut. The forces immediately diminish, to v and h. The stresses in the

Fig. 129 *(a) The depth of cut "d" sets up forces which cause a movement more or less in same direction as "Y". (b) The movement shown in (a) reduces the depth of cut, the forces diminish, and the workpiece deflection (now "y") changes.*

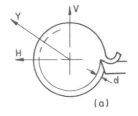 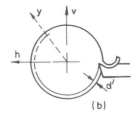

Work Steady Rests 91

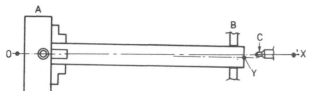

Fig. 130 *Effect of an incorrectly set steady rest. The center of rotation of the end of the bar is at "Y", so that the point "C" may be broken off.*

workpiece, previously induced by V and H, now cause it to spring back towards the tool. This restores the position shown in (a). If this process continues the work will tend to vibrate and if the forces and the deflections d and d' are 'favorable' to the natural frequency of either tool or workpiece we shall experience the phenomenon known as 'chatter'. To go into the mechanism of chatter in detail would need a book in itself, even more so if the many causes and remedies were to be explored. However, it is evident that if we can avoid the deflection of the work in the first place there can be no *variation* in deflection, so that the application of a steady rest to take up the cutting forces is an obvious course to take. Before leaving the subject, however, it is worth noting that a *small* variation in a *small* force is more serious than a *large* change in *large* forces, so that while a steady rest *may* be necessary during roughing, to ensure parallel cutting, it will be even more necessary when making light finishing cuts, to avoid chatter.

Overhanging Work

There are many cases where the cutting forces may not be very great but the workpiece overhangs from the chuck so far that its own weight may cause problems; or, alternatively, the overhang may result in such a loss of rigidity that chatter is likely. This can be met by the use of the steady rest. A similar situation arises when we need to center the ends of a bar too large to pass through the chuck. In this case we have

Fig. 131 *A model engine cylinder of some length being bored while supported by a steady rest on the top flange.*

Fig. 132 *Fixed steady rest in use when machining a bar 18 inch long which proved to be subject to chatter. The steady rest has bronze jaws.*

92 WORKHOLDING IN THE LATHE FOR HOME MACHINISTS

Fig. 133 *Traveling steady rest on the Lorch, machining 5/32 in. dia. stock 9 in. long down to 3½mm in a single pass. Depth of cut, 0.009 in. feed, 0.006 in/rev; speed, 750 rpm. This steady rest has hard steel jaws.*

an additional preoccupation; the forces may not be very great, but it is absolutely essential that the workpiece be held true to the lathe axis. Consider Fig. 130. This shows work held in a chuck at A and supported by the steady rest at B. The true axis of the lathe is OX, but the work will rotate about OY, because the steady rest is not truly set up. Several consequences arise. First, the work will be bent, and if it is stiff enough will 'work' in the chuck jaws – it may even work its way out. Second, if a center-drill is presented as at C it will be offset from the center of rotation of the work. At best it will drill a poor center, untrue to the axis, but more frequently the point will be broken off. Third; suppose the work to be bored or drilled. Then the bore cannot be true to the outside of the workpiece. Fig. 131 shows this situation, where a long cylinder, previously machined on the flange to provide a seat for the steady rest, is being bored.

Types of Steady Rest
Setting aside special-purpose and improvised devices, two types of steady rest are likely to be found in model engineer's workshops. The 'Three-point' or 'Fixed' and the 'Two-point' or 'Traveling' steady rest. These are shown in Figs. 132 and 133. The three-point has, as its first name implies, three supporting 'points' and is, as suggested by the more common name, fixed firmly to the shears of the lathe bed in use. The upper part of the casting is hinged and carries one of the three work supports, the others being carried in the lower half. The three supports are set in guides as a rule, so arranged that the points of the supports will meet at the lathe axis center when fully closed in. They are usually made of gunmetal or brass, the idea being that this is less likely to mark the work, but for many purposes hardened steel is better; it is less likely to wear during service, and a steady rest support which 'wears loose' is worse than useless.

The two-point steady rest (Fig. 133) is normally attached to the saddle, and traverses the work with it. It is set just ahead of the tool, though for some applications it may be set up so that it bears on the newly turned work. Two points are set, one vertically above and one horizontally behind the work, with the gap at the front to accommodate any projections around the toolholder. Clearly it has to be reset after each traverse of the tool.

Both types serve the same basic purpose – to resist the effects of the cutting forces – and in many applications either will be satisfactory. (Very occasionally it may be necessary to use both!) In general the fixed, three-point steady rest will be of most use when a long or slender workpiece is to be machined over a small part – e.g. it can be set up on the center main bearing of a crankshaft while machining the other journals. The traveling steady rest is, however, much more effective when machining the length of long work than is the fixed. It resists the forces very near to the point at which they are generated, and its use is almost an imperative when machining long screws – feedscrews and the like. But it cannot be used when the work has projections or shoulders. In short, both must be regarded as essential parts of the Turner's equipment.

Setting the Fixed Steady Rest

Setting up the fixed steady rest is not as easy as it looks, but let us take the easiest problem first – that of setting up to center the end of a bar held in the chuck. Assuming the chuck is reasonably true, start by setting the steady rest at the headstock end with the fixing bolt tight, and adjust the three guides or rubbers so that they all touch the bar. It is no use having the work rotating, for even if the chuck is true within 0.001 in. this will be enough to give a false reading. Once the three are touching, undo the top frame. Transfer the steady rest to the tailstock end, tighten down and close the top

frame, with a piece of cigarette paper between the two halves. At this setting, face the end of the bar. Now bring up the tailstock with a sharp center fitted. Compare the position of the 'pip' left on the end of the bar with that of the center; this will show whether the steady rest is truly set or not. Adjust as need be. Remove the cigarette paper and then tighten down the top half until you feel that the steady rest has a 'sliding hold' of the workpiece. Check the pip and the center again and then, if all is well, drill your center-hole. You can then reverse the shaft (assuming it to be unmachined, and thus the same diameter full length) and center the other end at the same setting of the steady rest. Naturally, if the steady rest is then required in the center of the same bar it can be moved to its new position without alteration of the jaws. This is, by the way, the 'preferred' method of dealing with barstock. Since both ends have been centered using the steady rest the center-hole will be as true as can be achieved.

Let us now suppose that we have a part-machined piece to set to. If held between centers then the steady rest can be set up in the desired position and a dial indicator used to see whether or not the steady rest is throwing he workpiece over. The indicator must be used both at the front and on top of the work. Again, I use the cigarette paper technique to ensure that the jaws are, in fact, properly contacting the work. If one end of the workpiece is held in the chuck the usual procedure recommended in 'the books' is to set up the steady rest close to the chuck and then to slide it along to the required position. Unless the chuck is absolutely true this will mean that the steady rest will hold the work offset by the amount of

94   WORKHOLDING IN THE LATHE FOR HOME MACHINISTS

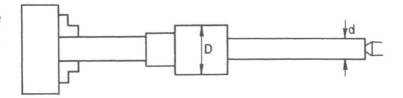

Fig. 134
How to set a fixed steady rest on work of stepped diameters. See text for details.

the eccentric error of the chuck. This may not matter, of course; an offset of, say 1½ mil will be of little importance if all you are doing is turning a short part in the middle of a long bar. The work will be round, and your micrometer will ensure that it is the right size. If, however, you are machining the length, then the work will come out taper by the amount of the chuck error. The proper way, therefore, is to set the steady rest at the *tailstock* end – if necessary reversing the bar in the machine.

If the workpiece is stepped so that the diameter at the steady rest point does not correspond with that at either end, then the dial indicator method must be used. Fig. 134. Measure the two diameters, 'd' and 'D'. Set the dial indicator at the tailstock end and adjust the cross slide so that the indicator reads zero. Wind back the cross slide by an amount equal to *half* the difference between 'D' and 'd', move the saddle to 'D', and adjust the steady rest so that the D.T.I. again reads zero. This sets the steady rest so that the work is held parallel in the horizontal plane. To set in the vertical direction, find a piece of packing that is nearly half D-d (or use feeler gauges) and use the dial indicator on the top of the bar, making allowance, of course, if the packing is not exactly half the difference between the two diameters. Fortunately the vertical setting is not too important, give or take a couple of mil. Just one qualification, though. If the diameter 'D' is likely to be affected by the chuck runout, then it is best to rotate the work by hand and take the mean of the readings.

Setting up for Boring
This is always a difficult one. Referring back to Fig. 131, the work will be held in the 4-jaw chuck and the first operation is to fit and center a lead plug in the bore, after which the tailstock can be brought forward to support it. Machine and face the flange.

Set up the steady rest with cigarette paper under the top frame closing face *and* between the two lower jaws and the work. Advance these jaws (one at a time) until the cigarette paper *just* tears when withdrawn. (This with the tailstock center in place.) Now do the same for the top jaw, and then remove the paper from the frame clamp and gently tighten down. To check that all three jaws are properly adjusted apply a little marking blue to the flange and rotate the work – only a few degrees; there should be a witness of contact behind each jaw. If one does not mark, adjust it very gently.

In many cases the exact adjustment of the steady rest may be less important. If, for example, a bar of fair diameter needs steadying (because of chatter, for example) it may be sufficient simply to set up the steady rest and press down each jaw by hand pressure – you will not move a 1½ in. bar very much, and if by chance the jaws ARE pulling it over the

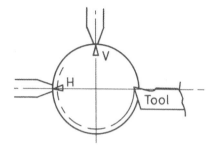

Fig. 135 *Setting up the traveling steady rest. See text.*

first measurement made with the micrometer after the cut will reveal this. Indeed, the final arbiter of ANY setting in the lathe, whether of topslide, tailstock, chuck, or steady rest, is whether or not the work is turned parallel.

Setting the Traveling Steady Rest
This is far less difficult. Even if the jaws are not exactly set the work will still be turned parallel, except as we shall see, at the very ends. See Fig. 135. The two jaws of the steady rest and the point of the tool form a 'three-point support' – one of which is the cutting tool. But the geometry is such that provided the cutting point lies on the work centerline and the two jaws touch at this center, only one diameter will fit. The cutting forces will (unless the steady rest is wildly mis-set) ensure that the work makes contact with the steady rest jaws. The qualification about the ends of the work is, perhaps, obvious. If the steady rest jaws are so set that the center of the work does not lie on the centerline of the lathe then, when the tool reaches the end of the work they will either force the workpiece off the tailstock or headstock center or there will be a gap between the jaws and the work.

Fortunately it is, as a rule, only in the center half of a long workpiece that a traveling steady rest is needed. (Though Fig. 133 is an exception.) It does not

Fig. 136 *Use of a steady rest when machining work which is longer than the lathe bed.*

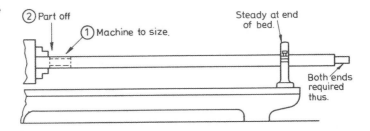

Fig. 137 *Procedure used in machining the ends of a shaft to fit bearings.*

matter too much, therefore, if the steady rest loses contact at the ends. This leads to the obvious conclusion that if we set the jaws at the end of the workpiece – again, using the torn cigarette paper as our measure – then it should perform its office when the critical part is reached. And so it does. The jaws may be set by finger-pressure alone, without the cigarette paper in most cases, but I always use it, just to ensure consistency of 'feel'.

It appears that there is some uncertainty as to whether the traveling steady rest jaws should be set to the work ahead of the tool or opposite the tool. The 'ahead' setting is the preferred one, for a number of reasons. First, the obvious one that the setting can be made before the tool cuts! Second, there is a little less risk of swarf getting between the jaw and the work – though care must always be taken to avoid this wherever the steady rest is set. Third, it is possible to remove any burrs from the work between each pass, which might otherwise interfere with the proper action of the steady rest. Here a special point should be made. When using the steady rest on long screwcutting operations (and this is where I find it comes in most useful) the steady rest – if it has bronze jaws, as most of them seem to have these days – may 'pick up' on the thread. In an extreme case I have known the steady rest start the carriage moving before the half-nuts were engaged. Remove all burrs from threads as you go along and, if you are wise, substitute harder jaws for this operation.

Stretching the Lathe

The fixed steady rest can be used to extend the 'between center' distance of the lathe, as shown in Fig. 136. The bar shown is 36 in. long, and the between center distance is only 19 in. on this machine. However, the full length can be machined except for the short length actually within the chuck jaws. In Fig. 137 I show an example of this type of job. The main body of the shaft did not need machining – it was for a countershaft and the 1 in. bdms was good enough as it was. The ends, however, had to be reduced to fit the available bearings. The stock was cut off about 2½ in. longer than needed, and set up as in Fig. 136. One end was held in the 3-jaw with a bit of paper under one jaw to correct the slight runout. That end was then machined to diameter and the shoulder formed with a knife tool. It was parted off at the chuck face and the shaft then reversed and the operation repeated. In that case the steady rest was set 'near enough' by adjusting it near to the chuck and then sliding it along; but if the full length is to be machined then it must be set using the dial indicator on the front face and

Fig. 138 *A boring collar in use. The stock will not pass through the lathe mandrel. The device is not as accurate as the fixed steady rest, but is much easier to set up.*

the top as previously suggested. There is, of course, a limit to what can be done in this fashion, but it comes in handy on the odd occasion when extra long jobs turn up.

The Boring Collar

This is a form of steady rest which is standard equipment to the Ornamental turner but seldom met with elsewhere. However, I found one with my Lorch precision screwcutting lathe and it does appear in a number of continental lathe-maker's catalogues, so perhaps it is worth a mention. See Fig. 138. It comprises a plate mounted by a central fitted bolt onto an angle-bracket machined to fit the lathe bed. Around the plate are set a number of tapered holes (included angle about 90 deg.) – in that shown in the photo they run from just below ⅛ in. up to ⅝ inch. They are carefully machined so that when indexed round they will lie exactly at center-height. When set up, therefore, a piece of barstock held in a chuck can be centered in the taper of the hole, and the end can be drilled and bored truly concentric. (The hole is set true by entering the tailstock center while the retaining bolt is tightened.) Its use presupposes that the end of the bar is faced – or at least reasonably true – and for small bars it is far easier to run the stock back through the hollow mandrel. But for work which is too large for this the device has its points; not least that it takes far less time to set up than does the fixed steady rest. It is hardly a piece of equipment that one would go looking for, or even worth making, but those readers who have really old lathes may well have one in their outfit and not really know what it was for! The 'Holtzapffel Addict' of course, will have a couple of really large ones, and be using them all the time!

Miscellaneous

As I suggested at the beginning of this chapter, it would be impossible to describe all the devices which have been used, or suggested, as work stead rests. Wood blocks set on the boring table and bored to suit the work (and presumably set to leave room for the toolpost) a similar block bored and attached to the lathe bed by through bolts, and so on; you will find them in all older books on turning. Most have their points and some are very effective. The important matter to be decided when considering any such unorthodox device is the purpose which it is intended to serve. If to reduce chatter, then my experience is that it is prudent first to try other expedients, and especially to look to the tool point and to the fit of bearings and slides. The test-bar seen in Fig. 132 suffered chatter when used in an old Drummond lathe I was overhauling until I diagnosed a springy gib-strip in the topslide, but it could be cured by setting a wedge of wood between the lathe bed and the workpiece. If, however, the problem is one of undue deflection under cutting forces, then simple wooden devices will seldom serve; a proper traveling steady rest is usually needed. However, there is no harm in trying – rather the reverse, for it is only by experiment that any true knowledge can be obtained! Just one final warning; the finger CAN be a most effective steady rest (damper, really) when incipient chatter is experienced in slender workpieces. But it is very susceptible to puncture by chippings, so interpose a piece of wood or leather between yourself and the work!

Conclusion

I have tried in this book to cover the basic elements of workholding in the lathe. (I do not regard holding jobs on vertical slides for milling operations as true 'lathework' – we have merely converted the lathe into a milling machine!) I am well aware of the gaps I have left; why nothing about wood-prong centers, or rubber bush collets, or divided driver plates for cutting multi-start threads? However, these are but special applications of either devices or principles I have covered already. One can fill the workshop with lathe accessories – and then spend a lifetime in using them to make more; it is that sort of machine tool! But there is one matter I have left to the end – though it

is implied in one or two of my remarks in earlier sections.

All machine tools are made to 'Tolerances'; they have to be, for if everything were to be guaranteed 'spot on' you would need to put in your Rolls-Royce in part exchange for a Myford and still write a hefty cheque. The guaranteed truth of a first-class 3½ in. center-lathe is 0.001 in. on the headstock center, and 0.002 in. in 12 in. length for the truth of the headstock taper. They usually come out better than that, but a machine having this order of runout would be passed by the inspector. (Even my Lorch precision lathe is guaranteed only to 0.0004 in. on the collet socket, though in fact the runout is half that.) So, a first class machine may be 0.0002 in. out in the headstock taper, 0.001 in. in 18 in. out on the bed, and have the tailstock poppet runout by 0.001 in. in 12 in. as well, when new. If you weigh it up you will realize that these tolerances are far easier to keep than those on a self-centering 3-jaw chuck with its scroll, jaw guides, jaw teeth, and all the other discrete parts involved.

For the type of work for which it is *intended* a self-centering chuck could run out by ⅛ in. and still serve, though it would be wasteful in material. I am afraid that we model engineers tend to use this chuck far too often, and expect far too much of it most of the time. A new lathe will come with a set of centers, catchplate and a faceplate, and ought to have a fixed steady rest, too, though this may have to be an 'extra'. With this equipment ONLY you can set to and make a model steam engine. However, I would start by making a set of screw-dogs for the faceplate and a taper mandrel to suit the bore of the flywheel etc first. You are then in real business, and can make a master chuck and a few slaves, which can be added to

Work Steady Rests   99

as time passes. Still studying 'what can be done' rather than 'convenience' I would next buy a 4-jaw independent chuck. With the addition of a tailstock drill chuck you can now undertake *almost every job of work that can be done* in the way of turning – with no self-centering chuck at all!

Why, then, all the fuss? The 3-jaw self-centering chuck will save a great deal of TIME. You can grip a bar, do all the machining, and part off the finished workpiece, all at one setting, draw out another length of bar and make another; and so on. If the chuck is running out 0.003 in., what does it matter? If it runs out by only 0.001 in., then that is probably as good as you could manage between centers, anyway, and as good as or better than you could manage with a collet adapter in the headstock taper. (Even collets are made to tolerances, too.) But the independent chuck will get the work spot on every time – if you *take the time* to set it properly.

If you have a 'Griptru', well and good – though you do have to set it up like you do a 4-jaw independent, after all! If you have a good chuck and have machined the backplate as previously suggested, then you can adjust this to run dead true – so long as it is new. But if you have the usual standard chuck direct fitting to the mandrel, what then? I hope by now that you will be able to distinguish between *repeatability* and *accuracy*. If a chuck is 0.005 in. out it can hardly be called 'accurate'; but if it is *'always'* 0.005 in. out and *always* in line with No. 2 jaw, then it is 100% repeatable; you know where you are, and all you need is a piece of 0.005 in. shim steel handy to set under that jaw every time you use it. 'Know your Chuck' – it may be repeatable by differing amounts at different jaw settings, but if you have a note of the various errors you can cope.

For all that, the inescapable truth remains; for accurate bar-turning you *must* work between centers, or on the faceplate for facing work; if the work is such that it must be gripped, then the independent chuck *must* be used – and if it must be *re-gripped* nothing else will assure accuracy. A master-and-slave chuck outfit will, if carefully made in the first place, assure accuracy also, but only on the work for which you have made slaves to fit. I have no doubt at all that you will continue to use the 3-jaw for most of your work, but *please* don't lose sight of the fact that though it may be the most used workholding device it is not, and cannot be regarded as, an accurate one.

CHAPTER 9

Lathe Alignment

The burden of the argument in the book so far has been to achieve the best degree of accuracy obtainable in the holding of the work. Clearly, all this will be wasted if the machine itself is not properly set up, and I propose to devote this last chapter to this aspect of the 'Art and Mysterie of Turning'. That some discussion is needed is without doubt, for there is a considerable degree of misapprehension shown in many quarters – even in reputable books on lathework. There seems to be a general impression that the object of lathe alignment is to set up the machine so that *the bed is without strain.* This is wrong – at least so far as small (3½ inch to 5 inch) bench lathes are concerned – though it is fair to say that a bed without strain *is* better than a machine which has just been dumped on a stand and set to work after simply bolting down!

To understand the matter, consider what happens when the lathe is being made. The bed casting will, after ageing, be rough machined and then, possibly after a further ageing period, all the working surfaces and holes except the final few mil on the bed shears will be machined. The underside of the feet will have special care to ensure that they are flat and lie all in one plane. The bed will then be set in a machining jig on the table of a grinding machine and the greatest care will be taken to ensure that there is no dirt between the feet and the table. The clamping arrangements will follow the principles which I have outlined in earlier pages to ensure that they *impose no strain* into the casting. The bedways will then be ground – in the case of raised vee-ways, with special wheels. Under these circumstances if the bed is now taken off the machine and set on an equally flat surface plate the Inspector will find that the ways are perfectly true within the limits of accuracy laid down by the quality controllers. The fallacy in the 'No Strain' method of setting the machine to work arises because those advocating it have forgotten what happens next.

After the inspection process the bed will be assembled with the headstock; the mandrel and other parts will be added – saddle, leadscrew, guards and all else. (I am afraid that I don't know in what order this is done!) All of this adds masses to places where, when it was being machined, the bed had none. But

Lathe Alignment 101

worse is to follow, and YOU are responsible! When you get the machine and have degreased it, almost the first thing that you do is to hang a huge (relatively) mass of metal on the back of the headstock in the shape of an electric motor. At a guess it will weigh about 25 LBf – more when the supporting bracket, countershaft etc is added – and its center of gravity lies perhaps 9 inches behind the lathe center. (One of my lathes, a 3½ inch center-lathe, topples over backwards if not bolted down, and it has only a ½ HP motor in place of the more usual ¾HP). This 'twisting moment' of some 250 lbf.ins is applied to the bed via the headstock and is *bound* to twist it. If you don't believe me, just lean on the tailstock when you are taking a fine cut between centers and see if this does not affect the chip; then consider what might happen if you were able to exert the same degree of leverage as is exerted by the lathe motor and countershaft.

The Lathe Bench

What we have to do in setting up the lathe is to introduce a strain in the machine which will *counteract* the effects of all the disturbing forces, and this we do by adjusting the clamping bolts which hold it down. That is why we have (as a rule) *four* such bolts, not the three which some misguided machine designers have used in the past. But we should start by using such means as we can to minimize the problem, and pay some attention to the stand or bench on which the machine is to sit. First, the top should be set as level as can be managed. There is, in fact, no virtue in 'level' so far as accuracy is concerned, but it does make matters very much easier when *using* the lathe, especially for milling etc, if we can set workpieces to a spirit level and be assured that they are then parallel to the lathe bed. If the stand is a metal fabrication, bolt it to the floor, and check with the level to see whether this

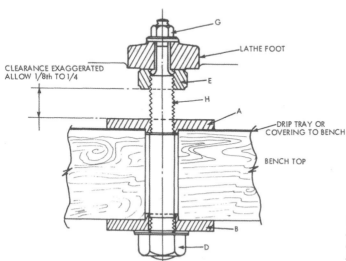

Fig. 139 *Jacking screws for setting up the lathe, shown here for a timber bench.*

102   WORKHOLDING IN THE LATHE FOR HOME MACHINISTS

act alters the readings across the seatings on which the lathe is to sit. If it does, set packing under one or other of the feet of the stand until tightening it down makes no difference. Note that you are not looking for 'split mil' accuracy at this stage, but the nearer, the better. If, during the process, you find that walking about on the floor alters the readings of the spirit level, then you must do something about that. In one workshop I had 40-odd years ago I had to set a couple of lengths of 6 in. × 3 in. scaffold planks on the floor to spread the load over several floor joists. This *is* important – if the floor moves under your feet it is possible to take off the odd half-mil just by shifting your weight from one foot to the other!

If the lathe is to go onto a wooden bench, again, get the top as level as may be. If you are starting from scratch, take care that the wood is well seasoned and has laid in the shop for some weeks to 'acclimatize'. Make proper woodworking joints, well fitting, and use glue as well as coach-bolts. And give several coats of varnish after you have finished it, to prevent it from moving with changes of humidity. Frankly, I find that a timber bench made in this way is actually superior to any metal stand, as the internal damping qualities of wood both absorb vibration and lead to much quieter running.

Jacking Screws

Now, having got the sub-base prepared you need something to hold down the lathe. Four dirty great woodscrews, washers, and a few wedges WILL do, but far better to do the job properly and make up some jacking screws. Secure the lathe temporarily and make up four screws as shown in Fig. 139. That shown is for a timber bench; if yours is

a metal one, then the washers 'A' and 'B' can be much smaller – indeed, 'A' could be turned from the solid – and, of course, the distance between them should be adjusted to take account of the dimensions of the stand top. For a timber bench make the washers about 2 in to 3 in diameter. The main body of the screw 'H' should be about ½ inch diameter for a timber bench, and at least ¼ inch larger in diameter than the part which passes through the lathe foot. The thread at 'D' should be the normal coarse BSW or 'M' thread, that for 'E' and 'H' the fine BSF or Metric Fine thread. The washer 'A' should be not too tight a fit to the thread so that it can level itself; and note the two bosses on 'A' and 'B' which locate in the enlarged hole in the bench.

Mark out for the holes in the bench from the lathe and then drill them, after which fit the washers 'A' with Loctite and tighten up 'D' and 'B', checking that the bolt 'H' stands vertical. As soon as the Loctite has set, slacken off 'D' again to be finger tight only. Run on the jacking nuts 'E' and mount the lathe, with the nuts 'G' run on enough to ensure that nothing falls over. Adjust the jacking nuts 'E' so that they take the weight of the lathe, and then pull up the nuts 'G' really tight. Make sure that this has not caused the reduced stem at 'H' to bind. (Incidentally, some users prefer to tap the top of the bolt 'H' and use an allen screw in place of the arrangement shown). Leave this set-up at least overnight, so that all can settle down under the weight of the lathe – this applies equally to metal stand or wooden bench. Then check that the machine can rock about on the stems 'H' reasonably freely – if not, then you may have to 'bump' the bolts at 'D' a

Lathe Alignment 103

Fig. 140 *Spirit levels. Behind – Semiprecision type with graduations on the glass. Front – Good quality carpenter's type, suitable only for rough setting.*

little to free it. You now have a machine support which gives you complete control over the alignment of the lathe; no packing, no wedges needed and you can re-adjust at any time if need be with no more than a couple of spanners. Those who own MYFORD lathes can obtain these jacking screws ready made, and incorporated in the standard 'raising blocks'. We can now proceed. There are several methods which can be used, and I will deal with them in turn.

(1) The Leveling Method

For this you will need a spirit level with a sensitivity of about 0.003 inch/foot. That shown in my photo Fig. 140 has a bubble movement of 1/10 inch at 0.005 in/ft, and is well within this; the carpenter's level also shown is not good enough, as the bubble shows barely discernible movement at 0.009 in/ft. If you have a level already, check it with feeler gauges at one end and if the bubble movement is definite at these limits, well enough; otherwise you will have to borrow one. Clean the bed and the foot of the level, and then adjust all the jacking screws 'E' until the machine is free from rock. Set the level *across* the bed at the headstock end and adjust the screws at this end to level. Set the level along the bed and adjust the tailstock screws until the bubble is again central – adjust on the *front* tailstock end jacking screw, following with the rear screw just to take up slack at this stage. During all this the holdingdown nuts 'G' should be slacked off and followed up with no more than sufficient contact to stop the lathe from walking about. Repeat the process once again.

Now tighten down all four holding down nuts to 'light spanner tight' – just finger pressure on the standard spanner. Set the level across at the headstock again, and adjust the front nut 'E' to get the bubble dead central; you will, or course, have to slacken and retighten the nut 'G' as well. The reading must be taken with this nut pulled up. Set the level *along* the bed, and repeat the previous exercise; then again across the bed at the tailstock end, each time taking the reading with the holding-down nuts reasonably tight, but with them slack when adjusting the jacking screw. You will soon learn how much to adjust to move the bubble a given amount. This process should be repeated at least twice and you may have to do it several times. Once you are satisfied, tighten the holding-down nuts fully and check again, readjusting if need be.

Your bed is now in exactly the state it was when on the finish grinder, and you can't ask for better than that. However, do remember that there is a *tolerance* on the flatness of the bed when it was made which is typically 0.00075 inch/foot. You should now use the machine for about a week and then re-check. Especially if it is mounted on a timber bench, or on a metal stand on a timber floor, you may find that it has settled a bit. I check my own lathes about once every 9 months or so, as the floor is liable to movement.

If your machine has raised vee guides, then you can either use accurate parallel strips under the level or, perhaps better, set the level on the *saddle,* for it is the vee-guide that you really need to check. In either case, if you find inconsistent results first, check the level itself by using it both ways round. Next, check that the level does not show a displacement when you walk about – you may have an unsuspected looseness in the floor. And, of course, that the level does not alter if you lean on the bench or stand! In both cases you will have to stiffen things up a bit before you can set the lathe up properly.

(2) The Dial Indicator Method
For this you need a dial indicator reading to 0.001 inch or 0.02mm; there is no need for one reading to tenths of mil. You will also need a parallel test bar, about 1 inch diameter and about 8 inches long with accurate centers. These can be bought – and they are very much cheaper than the spirit level of Fig. 140! – and you really cannot do without one for checking tailstock settings etc. However, you may find that the local Technical College actually makes these as exercises for their Technician and Craftsmen's courses and will have one they can spare even cheaper. Failing this, use precision ground mild steel, though you will have no centers in it then.

Thoroughly clean the mandrel nose and the threads on the self-centering chuck backplate and fit the chuck carefully. If you don't know which is the 'preferred socket' for the chuck key, check this now. Set the test mandrel in the chuck and the Dial Indicator (DTI) on the toolpost with the absolute minimum

of overhang. Apply the DTI to the bar as close to the chuck jaws as you can, disengage the bull-wheel from the pulley and rotate the chuck slowly, observing the dial reading. If it moves more than 0.003 inch send the chuck back, for it is out of tolerance – but first re-clean the threads and make sure there is no dirt on the scroll either. Now, slacken the jaws slightly and retighten at No.1 hole, noting the dial variation as you then turn the chuck. Repeat, tightening at No.2 key-hole and then again for No.3. The key socket which gives the smallest runout should be marked as the 'preferred socket'. This should be used in all future work with the mandrel. (However, you may have an old, tired, self-centering chuck. Never mind. Set the mandrel up with the *four jaw,* with shim between it and the jaws and set the mandrel running dead true in the usual way).

Now reset the DTI as accurately as you can at center-height where it touches the bar. Feed in to give about half the indicator travel. With the DTI close to the chuck, rotate the work and note the 'high' and 'low' positions with chalk on the chuck. Repeat this about 4 or 5 inches away from the chuck. The 'high' and 'low' positions should be fairly close to the same points. If not, then the bar is bent and you will have to get another – a bent bar is useless for this job. If all is well, then mark the chuck midway between 'high' and 'low' as being the 'Correct Test' position. With the bar in this position the DTI reading should be the same at the chuck and 4½ inches away. It won't be, and you must adjust the jacking screws until it is.

So, the procedure is as follows. First, using whatever level you have avail-

Lathe Alignment 105

able, get the bed level lengthways and crossways at the headstock as near as you can judge as previously described. Then use the DTI as I have described. If the free end of the bar lies *away* from the DTI bring the tailstock *front* jack UP; rear jack UP if it lies *towards* the DTI. Note that in this case all the work is done with the tailstock end jacking screws; those at the headstock should have been tightened down with the holding down nuts after leveling. The main problem with this method is that unless you are very careful and delicate with your adjustments you may find that you have been raising the tailstock end of the machine repeatedly, so that the bed is no longer level. Don't chase skylines; if the final reading suggests that the test bar is leaning *towards* the DTI by 0.0003 inch in 4½ in. this is as it should be. On no account, however, should it lean *away*. (Actual tolerance on a new machine here could be as high as 0.00075 inch in 4½ inches – 0.002 inch/foot, bar leaning towards the DTI).

This method can be made even more accurate – and simpler, too – if you have a test arbor with a Morse taper shank at one end to fit the lathe mandrel nose taper. This obviates all the risk of error which can arise from the tolerances on the chuck jaws. Such arbors can be bought – again, cheaper than a precision level – and can, of course, be made. *However, it IS imperative that the taper be accurate.* Any error here will be magnified and will give a false reading to the dial indicator. This is not difficult to ensure, but the fit of the testbar to the mandrel nose socket should be checked before you start. It should, of course, have centers in at each end – it can only be made properly between centers – so that it can be used for resetting the tailstock if need be.

(3) Turning test method

This is the final arbiter, of course, and I always use this method after applying No.1 with the level. After all, no matter what my instruments may say it is the result on the workpiece that matters. But it is rather more difficult to use as a *setting* method, though dead easy as a check. You need a micrometer reading to 0.001in. or 0.01mm and a piece of mild steel, preferably *not* BDMS, not more than 1 inch diameter (unless you have a 0-2 inch micrometer) about 6 inch long. You can use smaller, but I wouldn't advise anything less than ¾ inch. Set this well back in the chuck jaws and tighten well on the preferred socket – or set up in the 4-jaw if you like; it makes no difference. Take a cut along the length of the bar leaving two short barrels as shown in Fig. 141. This need not be a fine finish, but reduce the diameter by about ¹⁄₁₆ inch. Now resharpen the tool and, under power traverse and fine feed, take off just sufficient from the two test barrels to clean them up. Touch the tool with an oilstone and take a cut of 0.003 inch deep across both, again under power feed. Note, if you experienced ANY signs of chatter on the initial cleaning-up cut, reduce the speed. Measure the two bobbins with the micrometer. If the free end is *large,* jack up on the *front* screw at the tailstock end; if it is *small,* then jack up at the *back.* As before, if the free end is less than say 0.0003 inch large at this light cut, perhaps it is best to leave it as it is. Tighten up all the holding-down bolts and recheck. Fig. 142 shows this in progress.

It is not essential to use steel, but brass is expensive. Aluminum and its alloys tend to build up on the tool point. There is no reason why you should not use cutting oil, of course, but I

Fig. 141 *Test mandrel. See text.*

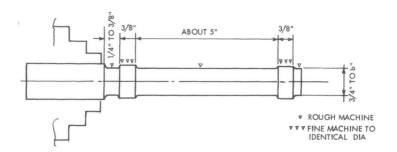

prefer to cut dry. My own tests are done on a piece of 'black' mild steel bar which cuts much more freely than bright drawn. Free-cutting mild steel is, of course, the ideal. One final point – keep your hands off the machine while it is cutting, for if you as much as lean on the tailstock it will upset the readings!

(4) Using Calipers
This will probably upset those readers who spend their time making workshop equipment, and who habitually use micrometers reading to 'tenths', but you *can* carry out test No.3 using a good pair of calipers! It is possible to *detect* a difference in diameter as small as 0.0005 inches with calipers. Indeed, during the 1914-18 war one munitions shop had girl inspectors who could detect a taper of less than 1 mil per foot *with their fingers*. Note that I say 'detect', not 'measure', but that is all we are really concerned with. However, you must use a good pair of preferably firm-joint calipers – not those with adjusting screws. If you don't believe me, take a fine cut over the bobbin, and set the calipers to it in the proper manner. (I will expand on this in a moment). Measure the diameter with your micrometer. Now just give a GENTLE tap to the cross-slide feedscrew handle and take another cut. It will be less than a mil, but I warrant that if you now offer your calipers you will be able to detect the difference in 'feel'. The 'proper' way to set them is as follows. To OPEN the blades, tap the heel of the hinge *gently* on some hard

Fig. 142 *A machining test in progress.*

Lathe Alignment 107

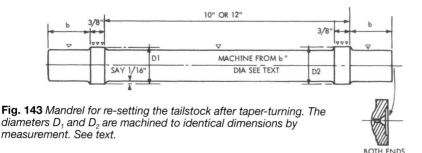

Fig. 143 *Mandrel for re-setting the tailstock after taper-turning. The diameters D_1 and D_2 are machined to identical dimensions by measurement. See text.*

surface – I use the top of my 4-tool turret; to CLOSE them, tap the back of one blade against the same hard surface. You can 'set' to better than half a mil in this fashion if you have a delicate enough feel to the job. Having reassured yourself on this matter you can set up the lathe with calipers in exactly the same way as just described using the micrometer.

Making a Test Bar

I referred in the first section of this chapter to the use of a test bar which had been ground between centers. However, it is possible to make one even on a worn lathe which will serve for many purposes, especially the vital ones of resetting either the topslide or the tailstock after turning a taper. See Fig. 143. I have one to these dimensions, made from 1 inch diameter bar. The piece is chucked at one end and the other held in the fixed steady rest for facing the end and making the center-hole. Note the profile of this, the little recess serving to protect the edges of the center-hole from burrs. The other end is treated the same way. It is then set between centers and a cleaning-up cut taken over the whole length – reversing it to deal with the part under the carrier, but this being reduced to about ¾ inch diameter for the 1 inch length. Again between centers all except the two 'barrels' or bobbins is reduced by about ⅛ inch on the diameter, and with a clean, but not necessarily a fine finish. It is worth making the distance between the two bobbins a definite length – say 10 inches.

Now take a fine cut with a well sharpened tool over one of the bobbins, using power traverse and aiming at the finest finish. Measure this diameter very carefully. Turn your attention to the other bobbin and taking even greater care, machine this to *an identical diameter.* If you go too far, then you must return to the other bobbin and remachine that one to match. The actual diameter doesn't matter (though it may help later to have a note of it stamped on the bar) but they MUST be exactly the same. You now have a test bar which can be used for resetting at any time, and which can be used for all resetting purposes. Note, however, that it *cannot* be used for setting up the lathe in the first place unless you are CERTAIN that the tailstock is correctly set. However, you *can* make a test bar for use with the DTI, by machining a mandrel identical to that shown in Fig. 141, but between centers and using the procedure outlined in making Fig. 143.

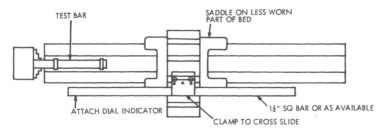

Fig. 144 *Arrangement for aligning a lathe having a worn bed.*

Aligning a worn lathe

None of the methods so far described can be used on a machine with anything but slight wear on the shears, as you cannot know whether the differences in readings observed are due to misalignment or wear. But there is a way out. It is in the nature of things that the amateur seldom uses this lathe for 'between centers' work – though I hope that one effect of this book may be to increase such usage. But most work is done from the chuck or faceplate, and this means that almost all the wear will lie in the six inches of bed adjacent to the headstock. This being so, we can set up the lathe by using the arrangement shown in Fig. 144. The test bar is set in the chuck as before, but the DTI is mounted on a substantial bar held in the toolpost. This allows the saddle to be moved over the unworn part of the bed.

Otherwise the procedure is exactly as previously described. Note, however, that the bar should be long enough to be clamped *in the middle* so that it does not tend to rock the saddle and bring the under-shear guide face into work.

A final note

Throughout the book we have noted that even light clamping forces can affect the accuracy either of the workholding device or even the lathe itself. *Every* applied force, no matter how slight, MUST cause a corresponding strain. *Every* force. Including that caused by your elbow when you lean on the tailstock, or rest your weight on the belt-guard while reaching behind the machine. I hope that this may persuade you to avoid such practices and, if your years weigh heavily (as mine do sometimes) then buy a stool!

Lathe Alignment 109

Index

Accuracy, conditions for, 11
  tailstock center 13
  lathe 101
  self-centering chuck 62, 67
Adhesives, use of 32
Alignment, lathe 101
Auxiliary collet chuck 85

Backplates 45
Balancing 40
Bell-chuck 71
Bell punch 16
Boring collar 98
Boring jigs 37
Button collet 85

Calipers, setting 107
Carriers 19
Centers 11
  types of 14
Centering work 15, 38, 49, 93
Chatter 91
Chucks, general 41
  attaching 44
  Bell chuck 71
  Cup chuck 71
  irregular shapes in 51
  Lantern chuck 74
  Master-and-slave chuck system 72
  Self centering 57
  tolerances on 62

Universal (independent) chuck 47
Wax chuck 76
wear in chucks 65
Clamping work 31
Collets, general 78
  adapter, No. 2 morse taper 86
  dimensions 80
  double-taper 85
  Myford 87
  stepped 83
Crankshaft turning 21

Dead centers 10
Dogs, faceplate 31
Draw-in collet 79
Driver-plate 31

Eccentrics, machining 67
Expanding mandrel 26

Faceplate, general 28
  dogs 31
  fixtures 35
Fixed steady rest 93
  setting 94

Gripping in a chuck 48
"Griptru" chuck 63

Jacking screws 103

"Keats" angleplate	36	Six-jaw chucks	68
		Square center	14
Lathe alignment	101	Steady rests, general	18, 90
leveling	104	setting	96
Lantern chuck	74	Stepped collets	83
Live center	10	"Stretching" the lathe	97
Mandrels	25	Taper turning	24
Master-&-slave chuck system	72	Test-bar, making	108
		Tolerances, self-centering chuck	62
Nominated chuck key	64	lathe	30, 106
		Traveling steady rest	93
Overhanging workpieces	53	setting	96
		Turner's cement	33
Raising blocks	104		
Revolving center	14	Wax chuck	76
		Wood, use of for workholding	38
Scroll chuck, errors	59	Wood-block chucks	75
strength	61	Worklength stop	87
Schaublin collets	83		

Index   111